The Best of my Grandmother's German Cookery

by

Carmen Graves

Editing and Typesetting by:

ProType, Ltd.
P.O. Box 49552
Colorado Springs, Co 80907
E-mail: protype@compuserve.com
Order this book
C. Werl-Graves Publications
1-719-460-2706
Fax: (719) 599-0764

Table of Contents

Foreword

Grandmother Ida was born in the Town of Breitungen, Germany, in 1906. Struggling against the harsh realities of living through both World Wars, she had to work very hard to make a good home in which to raise her son, Hans (my father).

Times were lean, so Grandma had to find new and creative ways to put nourishing—yet inexpensive—meals on the table. While some of her ingredients were found growing in nature, most of them came from her own garden. I remember her taking me out into the forests to bring out the natural flavor in our favorite dishes.

With both of my parents working, she was the only one mostly responsible for my upbringing. I frequently helped in the kitchen, gradually learning her simple approach to creating healthy, delicious, and easy-to-prepare meals. Today I am very thankful for that opportunity. Because of the years I spent in Grandma's kitchen, I am now able to pass her recipes and techniques on to you.

This book provides a broad assortment of authentic German recipes perfected by Grandmother Ida and by her mother before her. They include a number of basic German dishes, with which you may already be familiar. I think you will find them easy to prepare and delicious. I will also explain how to use a variety of kitchen herbs, all easy to grow in your own garden. And, finally, there is a "Grandma's Tip" added to each recipe to enhance your understanding of German food preparation techniques.

I hope you will enjoy and treasure these recipes just as much as my friends, family, and I have.

Happy Cooking!

Chapter 1

Using the Right Spices

MINT   THYME   PARSLEY   BASIL

Chapter 1

Using the Right Spices

For German cooking, it is very important to use the right spice for the right food. There are certain seasonings that are used only in small amounts because of their strong flavor, for example, garlic and nutmeg. Other spices can be used in larger amounts because of their mild seasoning qualities, i.e. dill, parsley, and chives. Such herbs give meals a wonderfully fresh taste and at the same time add a mild seasoning to the food. They can be grown easily in vegetable gardens and even in planters at a sunny spot inside the house. Dill, chives, and parsley are also very rich in vitamins, which is why you should always add them to the meal right before serving. Dried herbs, on the other hand, can be cooked with the meal for the last 15 minutes. Store dried herbs in airtight bottles or other airtight containers. Fresh herbs are usually best stored in Ziplock bags in the refrigerator. If you finely chop and freeze fresh herbs, you will always have fresh and tasty herbs right before serving a meal.

Aniseed (Anis)
This herb is used mainly in sweet doughs that have an aromatic taste, like cookies or cakes.

Basil (Basilikum)
This herb can be used in soups, salads, and meat dishes in small amounts. Basil is great with all tomato dishes.

Bay Leaf (Lorbeerblatt)

Never use too many bay leaves in one dish. Bay leaves are good in sauces, stews, sauerkraut, marinades, and some fish dishes.

Capers (Kapern)

Capers have a strong, picante taste and go great with egg dishes, fish, and some meat dishes. They also can be used in marinades and several sauces.

Caraway (Kümmel)

Caraway is a very strong spice. It is recommended for any kind of cabbage, sauerkraut, potato, meat, or cheese dish. Caraway is especially good for a healthy digestion.

Cheese (Käse)

You can use dried and hardened cheese as an excellent spice. Shredded or grated cheese is very suitable for casseroles, pizzas, soups, etc.

Chives (Schnittlauch)

For salads, vegetables, egg dishes, stews, sauces, etc., chives give meals a great fresh taste.

Cinnamon (Zimt)

Cinnamon sticks can be cooked with the food and are used in fruit and fruit purees. Grated cinnamon should be mixed with sugar (3 parts sugar to 1 part cinnamon) and used with pastries or just sprinkled on fresh fruit.

Cloves (Nelken)

Cloves are used in fruit desserts, apple purees, drinks (punch), red cabbage, and sauerkraut. Grated cloves are also used in gingerbread. Use cloves either whole or powdered.

Coriander (Koriander)

Use in meat and fish dishes, red cabbage, and savoy cabbage instead of nutmeg or cloves.

Cress (Kresse)

Cress is great with soups, salads, sauces, or slices of bread with butter.

Curry (Curry)

Curry is a mixture of different spices. It can be used for meats, fish, poultry, or picante sauces. It is a relatively strong spice and should be used in small amounts, unless you are using it in a main dish, such as curry meat, curry rice, or curry soup.

Dill (Dill)

Use dill for all types of salads, fish, eggs, stews, or dips made out of sour cream. Dill gives salads a great fresh taste.

Garlic (Knoblauch)

Be very conservative with the clove of garlic. Use garlic with gravies, stews, casseroles, and fatty meats, especially duck and mutton.

Ginger (Ingwer)

The dried ginger root is usually cooked in small amounts with pumpkin or other sweet/sour fruit purees. Ground ginger can also be used in souffles and for doughs such as gingerbread.

Horseradish (Meerrettich)

Horseradish is a very savory spice that can be used for egg dishes, cooked beef or pork, ham, sauces, smoked meats, and sausages.

Juniper Berries (Wacholderbeeren)

These aromatic berries spice sauerkraut, stews, and broths. Use them also with venison.

Lemon and Orange Peel (Zitronen-Apfelsinen-Schale)

Almost all sweet dishes, some drinks, marinades, and pastries could use some grated lemon or orange peel. The juice of the fresh fruit will also add a great flavor. If you grate fresh fruit peelings, make sure that all chemicals are rinsed off completely. To be safe, brush lemon and orange peel under warm water before use.

Lemon Balm (Zitronen Melisse)

Great with fish, meat, and mushroom dishes, ducks, herbal soups, and salads. Also use lemon balm with lemonades or other mix drinks.

Marjoram (Majoram)

Use marjoram with meat and vegetable dishes, soups, dumplings, potato dishes, or as an aromatic spice for cold meats.

Mint (Minze)

This spice is used in sweet dishes, some sauces, for teas, punch, or mixed drinks.

Mushroom (Pilze)

Dried and powdered mushrooms are used in soups, sauces, stews, and meat dishes. Fresh mushrooms can be used for mushroom gravies.

Mustard (Senf)

Mustard is used with meat, fish, cold meats, eggs, salads, and picante sauces. Also, you can marinade vegetables, cucumbers, mushrooms, and meat with mustard seeds.

Nutmeg (Muskat)

Use just a small amount in gravy, vegetables, dumplings, rice dishes, and some doughs.

Onion (Zwiebel)

Onion is a classic and healthy spice for every kitchen. Chopped onions need to be used immediately or they will lose their valuable nutrients and color. Use onions in a wide variety of dishes.

Paprika (Paprika)

Paprika can be used instead of pepper. It is a healthy spice that is made of grated pepper, in mild and spicy combinations. Spicy paprika is made of half rose and half sweet paprika, the mild combination is called sweet paprika.

Parsley (Petersilie)

Parsley is used in a wide variety of dishes. It gives almost any food a great, fresh taste.

Pepper (Pfeffer)

Whole peppercorns can be cooked with food, but grated pepper (both white and black) should be added toward the end of the cooking time. Pepper adds spice to broths, meat and fish dishes, soups, and certain salads.

Rosemary (Rosmarin)

Use rosemary with mutton, ragouts, sauces, and for herbal vinegar.

Sage (Salbei)

A strong herb for fish and meat dishes, soups, and sauces, use sage only in small amounts.

Sugar (Zucker)

Sugar is an indispensable ingredient for all sweet and sour dishes.

Tarragon (Estragon)

Use the strong flavor of tarragon in soups, sauces, salads, pumpkin dishes, roast, and especially to pickle cucumbers.

Thyme (Thymian)

Use in lettuce, fish and meat dishes, some vegetables, and venison. If you mix thyme with marjoram (3:1), the food will take on a peppery taste, especially in sauces, meat dishes, and poultry.

Wine (Wein)

Red wine is used with venison, beef, or pork roast. White wine is used with poultry.

Worcestershire Sauce (Worcestersoße)

This unique sauce can be used for meat, with mayonnaise, meat pies, patés, and ragout fin.

Chapter 2
Spreads for Sandwiches

Chapter 2

Spreads for Sandwiches

Aufstriche für Brot

Eggs (Eier)

As a general rule, spread butter on a sandwich first. Cut the hard-boiled, cold, peeled eggs into thin slices with a sharp knife or egg slicer. Top bread with the egg slices. Sprinkle with salt, pepper, finely chopped chives, and parsley.

Egg Spread (Eier Aufstrich)

2	hard boiled eggs
3	ounce butter
dash	paprika
dash	salt
1	tablespoon finely chopped chives

Cut egg white into small cubes. Blend butter until creamy and combine with egg white. Add salt, egg yolk, finely chopped chives, and paprika. Mix carefully.

Herbal Spread (Kräuteraufstrich)

4	ounces whipped butter or margarine
2	tablespoons fresh finely chopped herbs
	(such as parsley, dill, or chives)
1	teaspoon lemon juice
1	small finely minced onion
½	teaspoon marjoram
½	teaspoon basil
1	clove finely minced garlic
1	teaspoon paprika
dash	salt

Blend butter or margarine until creamy, combine with other ingredients. Blend again with wire whisk or electric blender.

Bread and Cream Cheese (Brot mit Käsesahne)

4	ounces cream cheese
2	tablespoons finely chopped chives
2	tablespoons finely chopped parsley
1	clove garlic, minced
1	teaspoon salt
1	teaspoon pepper

In a bowl, stir to blend cream cheese with parsley, garlic, salt, pepper, and finely chopped chives.

Bread and Picante Sour Cream
(Brot mit picanter saurer Sahne)

5–8 ounces sour cream
2 cloves minced garlic
½ small cucumber
1 teaspoon salt
1 teaspoon pepper

In a mixing bowl, finely grate peeled cucumber. Stir to blend with sour cream, finely minced garlic, salt, and pepper. This spread also tastes good with grilled veal and as a dip.

Other Bread Spreads (Andere Brotaufstriche)

Fresh Vegetables: These sandwich toppings go best with wheat bread or pumpernickel (Westphalian black bread). First, spread bread with margarine or butter, then top with either:

Tomato and onion slices, finely chopped parsley and chives, pepper and salt.

or

Cucumbers with fresh finely chopped dill, parsley or chives, pepper and salt.

or

Thinly sliced radish pieces with finely chopped parsley, pepper, and salt.

Otherwise, just combine different vegetables together on your sandwich, add some lettuce leaves and, instead of butter, use mayonnaise.

Chapter 3
Salads

Chapter 3

Salads

Salate

Salad Dressing 1

1	finely chopped onion
2	tablespoons finely chopped herbs (parsley, dill, or chives)
1	teaspoon lemon juice
1	tablespoon vinegar
3	tablespoons oil
dash	salt and pepper
dash	sugar
3	tablespoons water

In a mixing bowl, blend all ingredients together with a wire whisk and sprinkle with fresh herbs.

Salad Dressing 2

½	lemon, juiced
3/4	cup sour cream
½	small onion
2	tablespoons finely chopped herbs (such as parsley, chives, and dill)
dash	salt and pepper

In a mixing bowl, blend lemon juice with sour cream. Add onion, herbs, salt, and pepper and stir.

Salad Dressing 3

    1   lemon
    3   tablespoons oil
    2   tablespoons finely chopped herbs (parsley, dill, or
        chives)
    1   teaspoon sugar (optional)
    3   tablespoons water
 dash   salt
 dash   pepper

In a mixing bowl, drip lemon juice into the oil. Continue stirring until sauce thickens, add herbs, water, pepper, and salt. Blend together with wire whisk.

Salad Dressing 4

    1   tablespoon vinegar or lemon juice
    2   tablespoons finely chopped herbs (parsley, chives,
        and dill)
    1   cup sour cream
    1   small chopped onion
 dash   salt
 dash   pepper
    2   tablespoons oil

In a mixing bowl, sprinkle finely chopped onion with salt. Blend in sour cream, oil, vinegar, pepper, salt, and herbs.

Lettuce Salad (Koppsalat)

1	head lettuce
1	clove finely minced garlic
dash	salt
dash	sugar
1	tablespoon lemon juice
2	tablespoons oil
1	tablespoon finely chopped parsley
1	tablespoon finely chopped dill
½	finely chopped onion
2	tablespoons water

In a mixing bowl, combine oil, salt, sugar, finely minced garlic, lemon juice, parsley, finely chopped onion, dill and water. Blend everything together. Wash and slice lettuce into pieces. Pat dry and add dressing right before serving. Sprinkle with pepper, if desired. Serve with any kind of meat dishes or with bread.

Grandma's Tip: Keep some lettuce aside in case it won't be used at once, because lettuce will lose its taste if it sits too long in a dressing.

Yield: 4 servings

What's Important About Lettuce: Lettuce contains a lot of important minerals and vitamins. It is especially rich in Vitamin C. Right before using the lettuce, remove the outermost leaves. Rinse each leaf under water and drain. With paper towel, pat lettuce dry without squeezing the leaves. If the lettuce is still wet, the oil will not adhere. Mix dressing with lettuce right before serving, otherwise it will lose its fresh taste.

Celery Salad (Sellerie Salat)

2	large celery roots
2	cups salt water
2	tablespoons oil
1½	tablespoons vinegar or lemon juice
1	teaspoon sugar
½	chopped peeled apple
dash	salt
dash	pepper
4	tablespoons water

In a pot, bring water with salt to a boil and add washed celery root. Cook celery until tender. Meanwhile, in a mixing bowl, combine the oil and vinegar (or lemon juice) with 4 tablespoons water, sugar, and chopped apple. Take celery out of the pot, pat dry, peel and cut into thin slices. Slowly mix together with marinade and sprinkle with salt and pepper.

Grandma's Tip: If desired, add half of a sliced onion to marinade and sprinkle with nuts.

Yield: 3–4 servings

Radish Salad (Radieschensalat)

2–3	bunch of radishes
1	recipe of Salad Dressing 1

Cut cleaned radishes into thin slices and mix with Salad Dressing 1.

Grandma's Tip: Serve radish salad on a few leaves of lettuce. To make lettuce more tasty, sprinkle with a few drips of oil and lemon juice.

Yield: 3–4 servings

Spinach Salad (Spinat Salat)

½ pound fresh spinach
5 radishes
1 recipe of Salad Dressing 2 or 4

Rinse spinach leaves, cut into fine pieces, mix with dressing, and sprinkle with sliced radishes.

Grandma's Tip: If desired, mix marinade with 1 teaspoon horseradish, sprinkle with ½ tablespoon caraway seed, and drizzle with about 1 tablespoon juice of a fresh orange. Sprinkle with baked bread cubes.

Yield: 3–4 servings

Carrot and Apple Salad
(Karotten-Apfel-Salat)

6–8 carrots
2 apples, washed and peeled
dash salt
dash sugar
1 tablespoon lemon juice
½ cup plain yogurt
2 tablespoons raisins

In a mixing bowl, shred the apples and carrots. Mix with yogurt. Drizzle with lemon juice. Sprinkle with sugar, salt, and raisins, and fold together.

Grandma's Tip: As a variation, fold in 1 finely chopped celery stick and sprinkle with nuts.

Yield: 4 servings

Tomato Salad (Tomatensalat)

6–8 tomatoes
2 tablespoons mixed chopped herbs, such as parsley, dill, and chives
2 tablespoons oil
1 small onion, chopped
1 teaspoon salt
1 teaspoon pepper
1 teaspoon lemon juice
1 teaspoon vinegar
1 teaspoon sugar
4 tablespoons water

Wash and slice tomatoes. In a mixing bowl, blend carefully with a wire whisk lemon juice, sugar, salt, pepper, onion, vinegar, oil, herbs, and water. Fold into tomato slices.

Grandma's Tip: For variety, sprinkle with fresh basil. To make salad creamier, use 4 tablespoons liquid whipping cream instead the water.

Yield: 4 servings

Cucumber Salad (Gurkensalat)

2 medium-sized cucumbers
1 recipe of Salad Dressing 2 or 4

In a mixing bowl, combine thinly sliced or shredded cucumbers with dressing and mix together.

Grandma's Tip: Add 1 clove garlic, finely minced. Do not add any water, because cucumbers already contain a lot of liquid.

Yield: 4 servings

Cucumber and Pear Salad (Gurken-Birnen-Salat)

1   cucumber, peeled
4   pears, peeled
1   lemon, juiced
2   tablespoons raisins
2   tablespoons finely chopped almonds or other nuts
dash   sugar

Peel pears and cucumber and remove seeds. Cut into small cubes and immediately drizzle with lemon juice. Sprinkle with nuts, raisins, and sugar and carefully mix together.

Grandma's Tip: For a richer salad, add about 4 tablespoons liquid whipping cream and fold under cucumbers and pears.

Yield: 4 servings

Cabbage Salad (Krautsalat)

½   pound grated cabbage
2   tomatoes
1   apple, unpeeled
½   onion
3   tablespoons oil
1   tablespoon lemon juice
2   tablespoons liquid whipping cream
2   tablespoons water
dash   sugar and salt

In a mixing bowl, sprinkle grated cabbage with salt and mash with a potato masher. Cut tomatoes into small cubes. Grate apple with the peeling. Grate onion. Combine apple and onion with cabbage. Drizzle with oil and lemon juice. Fold in the liquid whipping cream with water. Season with salt and sugar.

Grandma's Tip: For variety, add 1 stick of grated carrot and fold into the salad.

Yield: 4 servings

Sauerkraut Salad (Sauerkraut Salat)

         1   pound sauerkraut
         1   apple
         1   onion
         1   teaspoon sugar
         2   tablespoons oil
    dash   salt

Put sauerkraut in a strainer and rinse under cold water. In a mixing bowl, combine the grated onion and chopped apple with sauerkraut. Sprinkle with salt and sugar and drizzle with oil. Carefully mix ingredients together.

Grandma's Tip: Fold 1/3 cup chopped pineapple cubes, 2 sliced radishes and, for better digestion, sprinkle with 1 teaspoon caraway seeds.

Yield: 4 servings

Bell Pepper and Cucumber Salad (Paprika-Gurken-Salat)

         3   bell peppers (red, green, or mixed)
         1   small cucumber
         1   recipe of Salad Dressing 1, 2, 3 or 4

Wash, clean, and cut bell peppers into small stripes. Combine with shredded cucumber and dressing of your choice. Carefully mix everything together.

Grandma's Tip: Do not use water in dressings, since cucumbers contain a lot of liquid.

Yield: 4 servings

Chapter 4
Salads with Cooked Vegetables

Chapter 4

Salads with Cooked Vegetables

Salate mit gekochtem Gemüse

Salad Sauce with Sweet Cream
(Salatsoße mit süßer Sahne)

½	cup liquid whipping cream
1	tablespoon vinegar or lemon juice
dash	salt
dash	paprika

In a mixing bowl, blend cream and slowly drip in the vinegar or lemon juice. Season with salt and paprika. Use this dressing for either cooked or raw vegetables.

Grandma's Tip: For variety, add ¼ shredded onion, dash sugar, finely chopped parsley, chives, and dill. Instead of using whipping cream, try buttermilk.

Salad Sauce with Oil (Salatsoße mit Öl)

2   tablespoons vinegar or lemon juice
3   tablespoons oil
dash salt
1   tablespoon chopped herbs (dill, parsley, chives)
3   tablespoons water

In a mixing bowl, combine vinegar or lemon juice with oil, salt, herbs, and water. Stir to blend.

Grandma's Tip: As a variation, add ½ finely chopped onion and 2 or 3 sliced radishes.

Salad Sauce with Egg (Salatsoße mit Eiern)

2   hard boiled eggs, separated
1   tablespoon mustard
dash salt
dash paprika
1   teaspoon sugar
1   tablespoon vinegar
2   tablespoons oil
1   tablespoon fresh chopped herbs (chives and dill)
2–3 tablespoons water

In a mixing bowl, finely mash the egg yolks of the hard boiled eggs and combine with mustard, salt, paprika, and sugar. With a fork or wire whisk, stir to blend. Drizzle with vinegar, oil, and water. Chop up the egg white. Sprinkle with finely chopped chives and dill. Carefully mix everything together.

Grandma's Tip: For variety, add ½ finely chopped onion.

Hollandaise Sauce (Holländische Soße)

1½	tablespoons butter or margarine
1	tablespoon flour
1	cup milk
1	cup water
pinch	salt
1–2	blended egg yolks
½	lemon, juiced

In a saucepan, melt butter or margarine and sprinkle with flour. Stir over medium heat until butter turns light golden brown. Slowly blend in milk and water. Bring mixture to a boil and simmer over medium heat for about 5 minutes. Blend in the egg yolks. Sprinkle with salt, drizzle with lemon juice, and stir. Serve with steamed vegetables, such as broccoli, cauliflower, or carrots.

Grandma's Tip: To refine sauce, add 1 teaspoon of nutmeg.

Yield: 3–4 servings

Cabbage Salad (Krautsalat)

1–2	pounds cabbage, washed and shredded
2	tablespoons vinegar or lemon juice
3	tablespoons oil
dash	salt
2	tablespoons chopped herbs (dill, parsley)
½	tablespoon caraway seed
2	cups salt water

In a pot with 2 cups salt water, bring cabbage to a boil and simmer for about 10 minutes or until cabbage is half cooked. Drain. In a mixing bowl, combine strained cabbage with vinegar or lemon juice, oil, chopped herbs, salt, and caraway seeds. Carefully mix everything together. To refine, use 3 tablespoons mayonnaise instead of oil.

Grandma's Tip: Add ½ finely chopped onion.

Yield: 4 servings

Cauliflower Salad (Blumenkohlsalat)

        1   medium head cauliflower, broken into pieces
        1   cup yogurt (plain)
        2   tablespoons tomato paste
        2   tablespoons oil
    dash   salt
    dash   sugar
        ½   onion, finely chopped
        3   cups water with ½ tablespoon salt

In a large saucepan, bring salt water to a boil. Add cauliflower and cook over medium heat until cauliflower is almost cooked. Strain the water and set aside. In a bowl, stir to blend yogurt with onion, oil, tomato paste, salt, and sugar. Combine with cauliflower. If desired, sprinkle with finely chopped parsley.

Grandma's Tip: For variety, sprinkle with about 1 teaspoon nutmeg. Another option is to use a vinegar oil dressing such as Salad Dressing 2.

Yield: 4 servings

Carrot Salad (Karottensalat)

        1   pound carrots
        2   tablespoons finely chopped herbs (parsley, chives)
    dash   salt
        ½   chopped onion
    dash   pepper
        2   tablespoons oil
        1   teaspoon horseradish
        2   cups water with ½ tablespoon salt
        2   tablespoons water

In a large saucepan, bring 2 cups salt water to a boil and cook or steam carrots until tender, then strain carrots. In a mixing bowl, combine oil with 2 tablespoons water, horseradish, herbs, and chopped onion. Sprinkle with salt and pepper. Mix together with sliced carrots.

Grandma's Tip: If you do not have horseradish, the salad can be prepared without it. For variety, add 1 tablespoon vinegar or lemon juice.

Yield: 3–4 servings

Bean Salad (Bohnensalat)

1	pound fresh green beans, washed
1	tablespoon finely chopped parsley
1	tablespoon dill
2	tablespoons vinegar or lemon juice
3	tablespoons oil
dash	salt
1	small onion
3	tablespoons water

In a pot, steam green beans in about 2 cups salt water over medium heat until cooked. Meanwhile, prepare salad dressing sauce with oil, vinegar, salt, water, and chopped onion. Strain beans, carefully mix with salad dressing, and sprinkle with parsley and dill.

Grandma's Tip: Blend 1 teaspoon sugar into the dressing. Instead of using fresh green beans, use strained canned green or yellow beans.

Yield: 3–4 servings

Asparagus Salad (Spargelsalat)

1½–2 pounds asparagus, washed
2 tablespoons lemon juice
3 tablespoons oil
1 tablespoon finely chopped parsley
3 tablespoons water
dash salt
dash sugar

In a pot with about 2 cups salt water, steam asparagus until cooked. Strain and cut sideways into 1 inch thick pieces. In a mixing bowl, combine oil with lemon juice, water, salt, and sugar. Fold dressing into asparagus. Sprinkle with finely chopped parsley.

Grandma's Tip: Instead of using fresh asparagus, strained canned asparagus is acceptable.

Yield: 4 servings

Brussels Sprouts Salad (Rosenkohlsalat)

1 pound Brussels sprouts, washed
3 cups salt water
1 recipe of Salad Dressing 1, 2, or 3

In a medium pot, bring water and Brussels sprouts to a boil. Reduce to medium heat and simmer for about 15 minutes or until vegetables are cooked. In a mixing bowl, combine strained Brussels sprouts with the salad dressing of your choice.

Grandma's Tip: As a hot dish, use a hollandaise sauce and hot vegetable.

Yield: 3–4 servings

Mushroom Salad (*Pilzsalat*)

1	pound fresh mushrooms
1	cup apple juice
dash	salt
dash	sugar
dash	paprika
1	teaspoon basil
1	tablespoon lemon juice or vinegar
2	tablespoons finely chopped parsley

In a pot, bring apple juice, salt, sugar, and paprika to a boil. Add washed, cleaned, and sliced mushrooms and simmer at medium heat for about 10 minutes. Drizzle with lemon juice or vinegar. Carefully mix together and sprinkle with parsley and basil.

Grandma's Tip: Add ½ finely chopped onion. Instead of using fresh mushrooms, use strained canned mushrooms.

Yield: 3–4 servings

Salad with Peas (*Erbsensalat*)

1	pound frozen peas
1	recipe of Salad Dressing 1, 2, or 3
3	cups salt water

In a medium pot, bring salt water to a boil. Add fresh or frozen peas. Simmer for about 10–15 minutes or until cooked. In a mixing bowl, combine strained peas and carefully mix with salad dressing of your choice.

Grandma's Tip: To serve peas as a hot vegetable, boil peas in about ½ cup salt water. Mix 2 tablespoons water with 1 tablespoon flour. Stir into the peas. Sprinkle with salt, pepper, and parsley. If desired, blend in ½ chopped onion.

Yield: 3–4 servings

Egg Salad (Eiersalat)

          4 hard boiled eggs
          3 tablespoons mayonnaise
          5 tablespoons sour cream
       dash pepper
       dash salt
          1 tablespoon finely chopped chives
        3–4 capers (if desired)
       dash paprika

In a mixing bowl, cut peeled eggs with a sharp knife into thin slices. Combine with mayonnaise, sour cream, salt, pepper, paprika, and capers (optional). Carefully mix everything together and sprinkle with chives.

Grandma's Tip: Serve egg salad with bread and butter. Sprinkle with fresh finely chopped parsley, if desired.

Yield: 3–4 servings

Meat Salad 1 (Fleischsalat 1)

        3/4 pound cooked ham
          1 small onion, finely chopped
          ½ tablespoon vinegar
          1 tablespoon mustard
          3 tablespoons oil
       dash pepper
       dash salt

Cut ham into fine cubes and combine with other ingredients.

Grandma's Tip: For variety, add 2–3 finely chopped pickle slices, 2 tablespoons mayonnaise, and 1 hard boiled, chopped egg.

Yield: 3–4 servings

Meat Salad 2 (Fleischsalat 2)

3/4	pound cooked, tender beef or pork roast
2	cooked egg yolks
2	raw egg yolks
1	teaspoon salt
1	teaspoon pepper
1	tablespoon mustard
1	tablespoon finely chopped parsley
3	slices of dill pickles
2	tablespoons mayonnaise
1	tablespoon lemon juice
1½	tablespoons oil

In a mixing bowl, mash cooked egg yolk with a fork and combine with ½ tablespoon oil. Stir in the raw egg yolk. Drizzle with lemon juice. Mix in 2 tablespoons oil, mustard, pepper, salt, and mayonnaise. Cut roast into fine slices and carefully mix with the marinade. Fold in chopped pickles and sprinkle with parsley.

Grandma's Tip: Instead of using roast, try cooked ham. Serve with bread and butter.

Yield: 4 servings

Chapter 5

Soups

Chapter 5

Soups

Suppen

You can use different broths (beef, chicken, or vegetable) to fix easy and fast soups. To thicken soups, use 1 tablespoon cornstarch to 2 cups liquid. Cornstarch must be blended first with about 2–3 tablespoons water and then stirred into a boiling soup. Prepare broth with a powdered broth mix following the directions on the package, or use a canned broth.

Rice Soup (Reissuppe)

Add rice, bread dumplings, and chopped parsley to any kind of boiling broth.

Vegetable Soup (Gemüsesuppe)

Add a variety of vegetables and chopped baked egg to a boiling broth. Simmer until done.

Semolina Dumpling (Griessklösschen)

    2/3 cup milk
      1 tablespoon margarine
   dash salt
   dash nutmeg
      1 egg
     ¼   cup semolina flour
      3 cups beef or vegetable broth

In a pot, bring milk and margarine to a boil. Add semolina, salt, egg, and nutmeg. Stir to blend with a wire whisk over medium heat until the dough is smooth. Scoop with a spoon into cherry-sized balls of dough. Bring broth to a boil, drop in the semolina dumplings, and cook over medium heat for about 10 minutes.

Grandma's Tip: If dough is not thick enough, just add some more semolina flour. Sprinkle with finely chopped parsley. Instead of using 3 cups broth, try 4 cups broth.

Yield: 3–4 servings

Dumplings (Semmelklösschen)

      3 tablespoons margarine
   dash salt
   dash nutmeg
      1 egg
      4 tablespoons bread crumbs
      4 cups beef or vegetable broth
      1 tablespoon finely chopped parsley

In a medium bowl, beat margarine until creamy. Combine with salt and nutmeg. With a fork, scramble the egg and slowly add to margarine. Stir in bread crumbs until the dough is firm. If dough is lumpy, stir in a few drops of water until dough is smooth. Let dough sit for about 20 minutes. Form small (cherry size) balls. In a medium pot, bring broth to a boil. Drop in dumplings and cook over medium heat for about 8–10 minutes. Sprinkle with finely chopped parsley.

Grandma's Tip: To refine dumplings, add about 1 tablespoon finely chopped parsley or chives to the dough. To thicken soup, fold in about ½ to 1 cup cooked rice.

Yield: 4 servings

———————— ⊰≈≈ɛɛ❮❮ɛɛ≈≈⊱ ————————

Herb Dumpling (*Kräuterklößchen*)

Add 1 tablespoon herbs (parsley, chives, dill, or marjoram) to semolina or breaded dumpling dough.

———————— ⊰≈≈ɛɛ❮❮ɛɛ≈≈⊱ ————————

Rice Soup (*Reissuppe*)

½	cup cooked rice
1	cup water
dash	salt
1½	cup broth
1	tablespoon finely chopped parsley
¼	of a chopped onion
2	tablespoons finely chopped carrots

In a medium pot, cook rice in salted water until done. Meanwhile, in another pot, bring broth to a boil. Add strained rice, onion, and carrots. Sprinkle with salt and cook over medium heat for about 10 minutes. Before serving, sprinkle with finely chopped parsley.

Grandma's Tip: Serve soup with bread and butter. To double the amount for soup, just use 1 cup cooked rice with 3 cups broth.

Yield: 2–3 servings

———————— ⊰≈≈ɛɛ❮❮ɛɛ≈≈⊱ ————————

Chopped Baked Egg Soup (Eierstich)

       2   eggs
       8   tablespoons milk
    dash   salt
    dash   nutmeg
       2   cups water

Blend all ingredients together. Grease a heat-proof cup with margarine. Add the blended ingredients. In a saucepan, bring 2 cups water to a boil. Set cup in the boiling water. Reduce heat, stir continually over medium heat for about 5–8 minutes or until egg stock is done.

Grandma's Tip: Egg stock is great to refine many different varieties of soups.

———————————

Carrot Soup (Karottensuppe)

       1   pound carrots, washed and lightly peeled
       4   cups beef or vegetable broth
    dash   salt
    dash   pepper
       2   tablespoons butter
       2   tablespoons finely chopped parsley

Cut carrots into 1 inch slices. In a pot, melt butter. Add carrots and cook over medium heat about 5 minutes. Sprinkle with salt and pepper, fill with broth, and stir. Cook over medium heat again for 20 minutes or until carrots are tender. Remove from heat and press everything through a strainer. Before serving, sprinkle with parsley.

Grandma's Tip: Instead of using 1 pound carrots, use ½ pound carrots and 1 or 2 potatoes. If you like carrots in pieces, do not stir them through a strainer, but carefully mash hem with a potato masher.

Yield: 3–4 servings

———————————

Egg Flake Soup (Eierstichsuppe)

4	cups beef or vegetable broth
2/3	cup milk
1–2	eggs
1½	tablespoons flour
dash	salt
dash	nutmeg
1	tablespoon finely chopped parsley

In a mixing bowl, blend egg(s) with salt, flour, milk, and nutmeg. In a pot, bring broth to a boil and slowly add the blended egg. Continually stir and cook over medium heat for about 10 minutes. Before serving, sprinkle with finely chopped parsley.

Grandma's Tip: To thicken soup, fold in about ½ cup cooked rice.

Yield: 4 servings

Basic Soup Stock (Grundsuppe)

2	ounces margarine
1	tablespoon flour
4	cups beef broth
1	small chopped onion

In a pot, melt margarine. Add onions and cook until transparent. Blend in the flour and constantly stir until golden. Slowly add broth and cook over medium heat for about 10 minutes.

Grandma's Tip: This basic soup stock is meant to be combined with other ingredients.

Yield: 4 servings

Cauliflower Soup (Blumenkohlsuppe)

Add cauliflower and herb dumplings to any kind of boiling broth. Simmer until done.

———◦◦◦◦◦◦———

Tomato Soup with Tomato Paste (Tomatensuppe mit Tomatenpaste)

    1   recipe basic soup stock
    4   tablespoons tomato paste
    2   teaspoons salt
    1   teaspoons sugar
    2   teaspoons paprika
    1   cup cooked rice or dumplings made of bread
        crumbs

In a pot, bring soup stock to a boil, combine with tomato paste, paprika, sugar, and salt and stir. Cook over medium heat for about 5 minutes, add either cooked rice or dumplings. Simmer for about 10 minutes. Sprinkle with finely chopped parsley or fried bread cubes. Salt to taste.

Grandma's Tip: Instead of using tomato paste, use only 3 cups water to 1 cup stewed tomatoes. Sprinkle soup with fresh, finely chopped parsley, or if desired, add some bread crumbs browned in butter.

Yield: 4 serving

———◦◦◦◦◦◦———

Tomato Soup made of Fresh Tomatoes
(Tomatensuppe mit Frischen Tomaten)

1¼	pound tomatoes
4	cups water or broth
dash	salt
1	small onion, chopped or sliced
3	tablespoons margarine
1	tablespoon flour
dash	paprika
2	slices of toast
2	tablespoon finely chopped parsley
1	teaspoon sugar

Cut washed tomatoes into small cubes. In a pot, bring water or broth to a boil. Add tomatoes, salt, and onion. Cook over medium heat for about 10 minutes. Mash with a potato masher. In a separate pot, melt margarine. Blend in the flour and cook until golden. Add the tomato stock, bring to a boil, and simmer at low heat for about 15 minutes. Stir constantly. Sprinkle with salt, sugar, and paprika. Spread toast with margarine and cut into 1 inch cubes. In a frying pan, fry toast until golden brown. Before serving, sprinkle soup with parsley and fried toast pieces.

Grandma's Tip: To remove peeling from tomatoes first, heat about 3 cups water in a pot, add whole tomatoes, and boil for about 1 minute. Now you can remove the peeling easily.

Yield: 4 servings

Cauliflower, Turnip, or Celery Soup
(Blumenkohl-Kohlrabi oder Sellerie-Suppe)

Prepare soup in the same way as asparagus soup, just add different vegetables.

Vegetable Soup (Gemüsesuppe)

        1   pound fresh vegetables
     1½   tablespoons margarine
     1½   tablespoon flour
        4   cups beef or vegetable broth
        2   tablespoons chopped herbs (parsley, chives)
   dash   salt
   dash   pepper
        1   sliced or chopped onion

Wash and cut up vegetables. In a pot, melt margarine. Brown onion slices, add vegetables, fill with broth, and bring to a boil. Blend flour with 2 tablespoons water and fold into soup. Reduce heat and cook over medium heat for about 30 minutes. Sprinkle with salt, pepper, and chopped herbs.

Grandma's Tip: Try the following vegetables for this soup: celery root, cauliflower, broccoli, green onions, carrots, celery, leeks, and 1–2 potatoes. To make soup creamier, remove about 1 ladle full of soup, mash with potato masher, and blend back into the soup.

Yield: 4 servings

Vegetable Soup with Beef Ribs (Gemüsesuppe mit Rippchen)

     1–2   pound beef ribs
        1   teaspoon salt
     1½   pound fresh vegetables, washed and cut (celery, carrots, leeks, tomatoes, cauliflower, green onions, or others)
        2   tablespoons finely chopped parsley
        4   cups beef or vegetable broth
        1   chopped onion
        2   potatoes, peeled and cut into bite-sized pieces
        2   bay leaves

In a pot, bring broth, ribs, and salt to a boil. Reduce to medium heat. Add vegetables, onion, and bay leaves and cook over medium heat for about 10 minutes. Add potato pieces, cover and simmer everything for another 45 minutes or until meat is tender. Take 2 ladles full of vegetables and broth of the soup. Mash with a potato masher and stir back into the soup. Before serving, sprinkle with chopped parsley.

Grandma's Tip: For a fresher vegetable taste, do not add vegetables right away. Cook soup over medium heat first for about 20 minutes and then add vegetables.

Yield: 4 servings

Asparagus Soup (Spargelsuppe)

    1   pound asparagus (white, if possible)
    3   cups water
 dash   salt
    1   tablespoon flour
 dash   sugar
    1   tablespoon butter
    1   tablespoon chopped parsley
    1   tablespoon lemon juice
    1   egg yolk
    1   cup milk

Peel and clean asparagus. In a pot, bring to a boil 1 cup water, salt, and asparagus. Add 2 cups water, reduce heat, and cook over medium heat for another 10 minutes or until asparagus is tender. Press everything through a strainer and put back into the pot. Meanwhile, blend milk with flour, egg yolk, butter, and sugar. Slowly add to the asparagus. Drizzle with lemon juice, blend with a wire whisk. If desired, sprinkle with finely chopped parsley.

Grandma's Tip: You can use canned asparagus, if desired. When using fresh asparagus, cut about 1 inch off the stem, which usually has a bitter taste.

Yield: 4 servings

Onion Soup (Zwiebelsuppe)

3–4	medium onions
1	tablespoon margarine
1	tablespoon flour
2	slices cheese
4	cups broth (vegetable or beef)
dash	salt, paprika, pepper, and sugar
2	tablespoons finely chopped parsley
4	slices bread (optional)
1	cup shredded cheese (optional)

In a pot, brown chopped onions in margarine until golden. Sprinkle with flour and stir rapidly over medium heat. While stirring, blend in the cheese. In a separate pot, bring broth to a boil and slowly blend in the onion mixture. Season with pepper, salt, paprika, and sugar. If desired, fill stoneware soup cups with soup. Sprinkle bread with cheese. Layer soup with toasted bread and cheese. Put cups in a preheated 350 degree oven for about 5 minutes or until cheese is melted. Before serving, sprinkle with finely chopped parsley.

Grandma's Tip: For better digestion, add about 1 tablespoon caraway seeds to the soup.

Yield: 4 servings

Hot Potato Soup (Kartoffelsuppe)

1¼	pound potatoes
1	carrot
1	stick leek, chopped
½	of a celery root
1	teaspoon caraway seed
1	tablespoon salt
4	cups beef or vegetable broth
1–2	ounces bacon
1	tablespoon finely chopped parsley
¼	cup liquid whipping cream
1	tablespoon cornstarch
½	finely chopped onion

Peel and cut potatoes into cubes. Clean celery and carrots. In a large pot, bring broth to a boil. Add potatoes, chopped celery, chopped leek, onion, and carrots. Reduce heat to medium. Sprinkle with salt and caraway seeds. Simmer until potatoes are tender. Mash everything with a potato masher or remove pot from heat and blend with an electric mixer. In a separate skillet, cut bacon into small cubes. Fry until golden brown. Add to soup. In a cup, stir to blend cornstarch with whipping cream. Bring soup to a boil. Fold in whipping cream and sprinkle with finely chopped parsley.

Grandma's Tip: If desired, remove two whole potatoes from the soup before mashing. Cut into pieces and add to the soup after you mashed the other potatoes.

Yield: 4–5 servings

Goulash Soup (Gulaschsuppe)

½	pound beef
½	pound pork
3	tablespoons finely chopped parsley
3	tomatoes
1	onion
1	bell pepper
5	cups beef broth
2	tablespoons flour
1	peeled potato
2	teaspoons caraway seeds
1½	tablespoons margarine
dash	salt

Rinse meat, pat dry, and cut into small cubes. In a pot, melt margarine. Sprinkle with flour and salt. Brown meat in the flour mixture until golden. Cut onion, tomatoes, potato, and bell pepper into small cubes and add to meat. Add 1 cup broth, sprinkle with caraway seeds, and cook over medium heat for 10 minutes. Slowly blend in the remainder of the broth. Over medium, simmer for 30–45 minutes. Mash with potato masher. Before serving, sprinkle with finely chopped parsley.

Grandma's Tip: Serve soup with bread and butter. Instead of using a mixture of beef and pork, select only one kind of meat. If you want soup with more meat, just cook another ½ pound meat with soup. For a richer soup, stir in about 2 tablespoons liquid whipping cream.

Yield: 4 servings

Mushroom Soup (Pilzsuppe)

½	pound mushrooms (finely minced)
1	tablespoon flour
4	cups chicken broth
1/3	cup liquid whipping cream
dash	salt
dash	paprika
1	tablespoon finely chopped parsley
1	egg yolk
dash	nutmeg
1	tablespoon margarine

Wash mushrooms and chop into fine pieces (use a rocking chopper, if available). In a pot, melt margarine, add mushrooms, and brown for about 10 minutes over medium heat. Sprinkle with flour, salt, nutmeg, and paprika. Slowly add the boiling broth. Cook over medium heat for about 20 minutes. Blend in the egg yolk and liquid whipping cream. Before serving, sprinkle with finely chopped parsley.

Grandma's Tip: For variety, add ½ finely minced onion. Instead of using fresh mushrooms, you also could use canned, strained mushrooms.

Yield: 4 servings

Bean, Pea, or Lentil Soup
(Bohnen-Erbsen oder Linsen-Suppe)

1	cup beans, peas, or lentils
5	cups and 3 tablespoons broth or water
¼	pound bacon
1	tablespoon salt
1	tablespoon vinegar
1	tablespoon flour
1	medium onion
1	tablespoon chopped parsley (optional)
1	teaspoon marjoram

In a pot, mix water or broth with beans, peas, or lentils and simmer over low heat for about 1 hour. Combine with bacon, salt, finely chopped onion, and marjoram. Cook over medium heat for 20 minutes. Remove bacon and cut into small pieces. Blend 3 tablespoons water with flour. Bring soup to a boil and stir into soup. Also fold in the bacon pieces. Simmer for another 20 minutes. Blend in the vinegar and, before serving, sprinkle with finely chopped parsley.

Grandma's Tip: If soup will be reheated, do not blend in the vinegar, just add it right before serving. Smoked sausages are a nice addition to the soup. Add them to the soup about 20 minutes before serving.

Yield: 4–5 servings

Chapter 6

Sauces

Chapter 6

Sauces

———————◦◦◦€€€€€◦◦◦———————

Soßen

Sauces usually complete the taste of most dishes. There is more to sauce making than simply flour, water, salt, and pepper. Here are some tips for making a sauce richer. The liquid for sauce can be water, juice, milk, meat, or vegetable broth. If you like to use cornstarch or flour to thicken the sauce, combine it with a few tablespoons of cold water before mixing into the boiling liquid. For variety, use a white wine for white sauces or red wine for dark sauces. Sweet cream, butter, and egg yolk will refine any sauce. Adding egg yolk to a white sauce gives it a great color. Do not cook fresh herbs, horseradish, lemon juice, or mustard during the cooking process. Add those ingredients just before serving.

———————◦◦◦€€€€◦◦◦———————

Basic White Sauce (Weiße Grundsoße)

2	tablespoons butter
1	tablespoon flour
2	cups milk
dash	salt

In a large saucepan, melt butter. Add flour and stir until golden brown. Slowly stir in the cold milk and boil for a few minutes. Season with salt or other spices, as desired.

Yield: 4 servings

———————◦◦◦€€€€◦◦◦———————

Basic Dark Sauce (Braune Grundsoße)

            2   tablespoons butter
            1   tablespoon flour
          ½   onion, chopped
            2   cups beef broth
      dash   salt
      dash   pepper

In a large saucepan, melt butter and brown onion until transparent. Sprinkle with flour. Blend in the broth and sprinkle with salt and pepper. Stir and cook over medium heat for about 15 minutes.

Grandma's Tip: Slowly blend in the broth with a wire whisk so that flour dissolves.

Yield: 4 servings

Herbal Sauce (Kräutersoße)

            1   recipe of sauce
            3   tablespoons finely chopped herbs (parsley, chives, dill, basil)
            1   teaspoon lemon juice
            1   egg yolk
      dash   salt
      dash   pepper

In a saucepan, prepare basic white sauce. Reduce heat, blend in the egg yolk. Combine with finely chopped herbs. Drizzle with lemon juice and sprinkle with salt and pepper.

Grandma's Tip: Serve with noodles, rice, or potatoes. This sauce is great in a noodle or potato casserole.

Yield: 4 servings

Onion Sauce (Zwiebelsoße)

> 2 cups beef broth
> 1 tablespoon finely chopped parsley
> 2 tablespoons butter or margarine
> 1 tablespoon flour
> 1 medium-sized onion, finely chopped
> dash salt
> dash basil (optional)
> dash pepper
> ½ tablespoon caraway seed

In a pot, melt margarine and brown onions until transparent. Add flour. Slowly fill with broth and bring to a boil. Reduce heat. Sprinkle with salt, pepper, basil, and caraway seeds. Stir together and cook over medium heat for about 10 minutes. Sprinkle with finely chopped parsley.

Grandma's Tip: To refine the sauce, add 1–2 bay leaves. Serve over chops or steaks.

Yield: 4 servings

Caraway Sauce (Kümmelsoße)

> 1 recipe dark sauce stock
> 1–2 tablespoons caraway seeds
> dash salt
> dash pepper
> dash basil (optional)

In a pot, prepare basic sauce stock. Combine with caraway seeds, salt, pepper, and basil (optional). Bring everything to a boil and cook over medium heat for about 10 minutes.

Grandma's Tip: Serve this sauce with a sauerkraut/potato dish, or try it with a fried meat.

Yield: 4 servings

Bechamel Sauce (Béchamelsoße)

¼	pound bacon
1	medium onion, finely chopped
2	cups milk
2	tablespoons liquid whipping cream
2	tablespoons shredded cheese
dash	salt
dash	paprika
½	tablespoon lemon juice (optional)
1	tablespoon flour
2	tablespoons water

Cut bacon into small cubes. In a pot, fry the bacon until light golden. Add the onions and strain the grease. Blend in the milk, whipping cream, cheese, salt, and paprika. Bring to a boil. Mix 2 tablespoons water with the flour and blend into sauce. Reduce heat and cook over medium heat for about 20 minutes. Drizzle with lemon juice.

Grandma's Tip: Instead of using bacon, try smoked ham or bologna. To refine the sauce, blend in 1 egg yolk. Serve over noodles and sprinkle with parsley.

Yield: 4 servings

Caper Sauce (Kapernsoße)

1	recipe white sauce stock
2	tablespoons capers
1	tablespoon mustard
1	tablespoon vinegar

Mash up capers and add to white sauce stock. Season with mustard and vinegar. Fold together and cook over medium heat for about 10 minutes.

Grandma's Tip: This sauce is great with egg and potato dishes. To bring out the taste of the capers, mash 1 tablespoon of the capers.

Yield: 4 servings

Horseradish Sauce (Meerrettichsoße)

1	recipe white sauce stock
2	tablespoons shredded horseradish
1	tablespoon lemon juice or vinegar
dash	sugar
2	tablespoons liquid whipping cream
dash	salt

In a pot, bring white sauce stock to a boil. Reduce heat, blend in the whipping cream and horseradish. Drizzle with lemon juice. Sprinkle with sugar and salt. Fold together and cook over medium heat for about 20 minutes.

Grandma's Tip: This sauce is really good with potatoes and fish. To make sauce creamier, blend in 2 more tablespoons of liquid whipping cream.

Yield: 4 servings

Hollandaise Sauce (Holländische Soße)

1	recipe white sauce stock
1–2	blended eggs
½	lemon
dash	nutmeg
dash	salt

Make white sauce stock and slowly stir in blended eggs. Add lemon juice and nutmeg. Cook over medium heat about 10 minutes.

Grandma's Tip: If you would like to use this sauce with a chicken dish, use 1 part chicken broth to 1 part milk. Sauce is great with vegetable dishes.

Yield: 4 servings

Cheese Sauce (Käsesoße)

   1   recipe white sauce, cooked
   2   ounces shredded cheese
   1   tablespoon lemon juice

Add shredded cheese to prepared white sauce. Add the lemon juice and cook over medium heat for about 10 minutes.

Grandma's Tip: Cheese sauce goes great with broccoli and cauliflower dishes. Blend cheese rapidly into the sauce. If desired, add 1 tablespoon butter.

Yield: 4 servings

Curry Sauce (Currysoße)

   1   recipe white sauce stock made with 1 part water and 1 part milk
   1   tablespoon curry powder
   1   small onion, finely chopped
   1   teaspoon ginger
   1   tablespoon lemon juice

Prepare white sauce and add curry powder, onion, and ginger. Cook over medium heat for about 10 minutes. Blend in the lemon juice.

Grandma's Tip: Instead of using ginger, add 1 tablespoon mustard, 1 tablespoon ketchup, and use water instead of milk. Mix 1 package brown gravy mix with 2 cups water. Blend in 2 tablespoons sour cream. This sauce goes great with a bratwurst.

Yield: 4 servings

Mustard Sauce (Senfsoße)

1 recipe white sauce stock
3 tablespoons mustard
1 tablespoon vinegar
1 teaspoon sugar

Make white sauce and stir in mustard, vinegar, and sugar. Cook over medium heat for about 10 minutes.

Grandma's Tip: This sauce is great with fish dishes. Drizzle with lemon juice, if desired.

Yield: 4 servings

Tomato Sauce (Tomatensoße)

1 recipe white sauce
4 tablespoons tomato paste
1 medium onion, finely chopped
1 teaspoon sugar
1 tablespoon vinegar
1 teaspoon pepper
1 teaspoon salt

Add tomato paste and onion to white sauce. Bring to a boil. Season with sugar, salt, pepper, and vinegar. Cook over medium heat for about 15 minutes.

Grandma's Tip: If desired, stir in 2 tablespoons ketchup. To refine, add butter, chopped ham, or bologna. Add 1–2 tablespoons fresh finely chopped parsley and sprinkle with basil. Serve this sauce with noodles.

Yield: 4 servings

Sauce with Bacon (Soße mit Speck)

¼ pound bacon
1 medium finely chopped onion
1 teaspoon pepper
1 tablespoon flour
1 teaspoon salt
1 teaspoon powdered cloves
1 teaspoon vinegar
1 teaspoon sugar
2 cups beef broth

Chop bacon into small cubes. In a pot, brown the bacon with chopped onion until golden. Strain the grease. Sprinkle with flour and stir. Slowly add the broth and bring to a boil. Sprinkle with salt, pepper, clove powder, and sugar. Drizzle with vinegar and cook over medium heat for about 10 minutes.

Grandma's Tip: Blend sauce well with a wire whisk. Serve with noodles or pour over fried breaded pork chops.

Yield: 4 servings

Red Wine Sauce (Rotweinsoße)

1 recipe dark sauce
1 teaspoon salt
1 teaspoon pepper
1 teaspoon sugar
2/3 cup red wine

Make dark sauce. Add salt, pepper, and sugar. Bring to a boil and blend in the red wine. Reduce heat to medium and cook for about 15 minutes.

Grandma's Tip: For variety, add 3–5 peppercorns and drizzle with lemon juice. Serve this sauce with venison.

Yield: 4 servings

Raisin Sauce (Rosinensoße)

1 recipe brown sauce
2 ounces raisins
1 tablespoon chopped almonds
1 pinch clove powder (or 2–4 whole cloves)
1 teaspoon sugar
1 teaspoon lemon juice

Add raisins, almonds, clove, sugar, and lemon juice to brown sauce. Bring to a boil and cook over medium heat for about 10 minutes.

Grandma's Tip: As a variation, use 2 tablespoons red wine, instead of lemon juice. To serve with poultry, use a white sauce instead of brown sauce. Otherwise serve with meat dishes.

Yield: 4 servings

Mushroom Sauce (Pilzsoße)

1 recipe brown sauce
1 cup finely chopped fresh mushrooms or strained canned mushrooms
1 tablespoon butter
1 teaspoon salt
1 teaspoon paprika
1 tablespoon finely chopped parsley

In a saucepan, melt butter and brown mushrooms until golden. In a pot, bring dark sauce to a boil. Add mushrooms and cook over medium heat for about 20 minutes. Sprinkle with salt, paprika, and parsley. Stir and simmer for another 10 minutes.

Grandma's Tip: To make this sauce creamier, add 2 tablespoons liquid whipping cream. Serve with chops, steaks, or noodle dishes.

Yield: 4 servings

Cold Mustard Sauce (Kalte Senfsoße)

     2   anchovies
     2   small finely chopped onions
     2   yolks of boiled eggs
     2   tablespoons finely chopped parsley
     2   tablespoons mustard
     2   tablespoons lemon juice or vinegar
     3   tablespoons oil
  dash   salt
  dash   sugar
  dash   paprika

Finely chop anchovies, onions, and egg yolks. Mix with the other ingredients in a bowl.

Grandma's Tip: Use this sauce as a dip for any kind of fish or fish sticks. Great for making deviled eggs.

Yield: 4 servings

Fondue Sauce (Fondue Soße)

     4   tablespoons cranberry sauce
     3   tablespoons mustard
     1   teaspoon lemon juice or vinegar
  dash   paprika
     1   fine shredded onion

In a bowl, blend all ingredients with a fork or wire whisk.

Grandma's Tip: Serve this sauce with meat or chicken. For variety, add shredded melted cheese. Try dipping cheese balls: Make balls of Camembert cheese. Dip in 1 blended egg and roll in plain bread crumbs. Fry in melted butter on both sides until golden brown and inside of cheese is melted.

Yield: 4 servings

Yogurt Sauce (Yoghurtsoße)

    1 cup plain yogurt
    1 tablespoon lemon juice
    1 tablespoon sugar
 dash salt
    2 tablespoons mayonnaise
    2 tablespoons fresh chopped herbs (parsley, dill, etc.)

In a bowl, blend yogurt, salt, sugar, lemon juice, and mayonnaise until creamy. Add fresh herbs and stir.

Grandma's Tip: If desired, blend in 1 tablespoon ketchup or tomato paste. Instead of using yogurt, try sour cream. This sauce is great as a vegetable dip.

Yield: 4 servings

Tarter Sauce (Tartarsoße)

    1 cup mayonnaise
    1 teaspoon finely chopped onion
    2 tablespoons minced bell pepper
    2 tablespoons finely chopped capers
    1 tablespoons finely chopped parsley
    1 teaspoon lemon juice

In a bowl, blend mayonnaise with onions, bell pepper, capers and parsley. Season with lemon juice and stir again.

Grandmas Tip: If desired, blend in 1–2 pieces finely chopped anchovy fillets. Serve as a filling for deviled eggs, as a sauce for fish, or as a dip.

Yield: 4 servings

Butter Sauce (Buttersoße)

         2   egg yolks
         1   teaspoon salt
         1   teaspoon pepper
         1   teaspoon vinegar or lemon juice
        ½   cup melted butter
         1   cup water

In a large saucepan, heat the water. In a large cup, blend egg yolks, salt, pepper, melted butter, and vinegar. Set cup into the heated water. Stir ingredients and simmer over medium heat for about 10 minutes or until the egg yolk thickens.

Grandma's Tip: This sauce is used only in small amounts for garnishing roast beef or asparagus.

Yield: 4 servings

Horseradish Cream Sauce (Meerrettich-Krem-Soße)

       2/3   cups whipping cream
         1   shredded apple
         2   tablespoons horseradish
         1   teaspoon lemon juice
         1   teaspoon sugar
         1   teaspoon salt

In a bowl, beat whipping cream until stiff. In a separate bowl, stir together shredded apple, horseradish, lemon juice, sugar, and salt. Fold in the whipping cream.

Grandma's Tip: Serve this sauce right away or freeze. Use as a vegetable dip or for cheese or meat fondues.

Yield: 4 servings

Vanilla Milk (Vanille Milch)

    2   cups milk
    ¼   cup sugar
    1   tablespoon vanilla extract

In a pot, bring milk to a boil. Blend in the sugar and vanilla extract. Cook over medium heat for about 5 minutes, stirring continuously. Serve cold.

Grandma's Tip: This milk tastes especially good cold. It is a refreshing milk drink.

Yield: 2 servings

Vanilla Sauce (Vanillesoße)

       2   cups milk
       2   tablespoons sugar
       1   teaspoon vanilla extract
    dash   salt
       1   tablespoon cornstarch
       1   egg yolk

In a pot, bring 1½ cup milk, sugar, vanilla extract, and salt to a boil and reduce heat. In a bowl, blend ½ cup milk with cornstarch. Bring the first milk mixture to a boil again and blend cornstarch mixture into the boiling milk. Reduce heat and fold in the egg yolk. Simmer over low heat for another 3–5 minutes.

Grandma's Tip: Hot vanilla sauce is great for a variety of fresh fruit, fruit stews, or dumplings.

Yield: 4 servings

Almond Sauce (Mandelsoße)

Use vanilla sauce recipe, but instead of using vanilla extract use 1 teaspoon almond extract. If desired, blend in 2 tablespoons shredded almonds.

———————⊳∝∝€€€∝∝⊲———————

Caramel Sauce (Karamelsoße)

½ cup sugar
2/3 cup water
2 cup milk
1 tablespoon cornstarch
dash salt

In a saucepan, add the sugar and stir continually over low heat until golden brown. Slowly blend in the water. In a separate pot, bring 1½ cups milk to a boil. Remove from heat and slowly stir into the sugar water. Meanwhile in a bowl, blend rest of the milk with cornstarch and salt. Bring milk to a boil and blend in the milk mixed with cornstarch (stir rapidly with a wire whisk).

Grandma's Tip: This sauce is usually served as vanilla pudding or with fruits. For a richer sauce, blend in 1–2 egg yolks.

Yield: 4 servings

———————⊳∝∝€€€∝∝⊲———————

Chocolate Sauce (Schokoladensoße)

        2   cups milk
        ¼   cup sugar
        2   tablespoons cocoa
        1   tablespoon cornstarch

In a pot, bring 1½ cups milk to a boil, then remove from stove. In a bowl, stir to blend ½ cup milk with sugar, cocoa, and cornstarch. Stir into the hot milk. Bring to a boil again and cook over medium heat for another 5 minutes.

Grandma's Tip: Instead of cocoa, use 4 tablespoons shredded real chocolate. Use this sauce as topping for puddings or fruits.

Yield: 4 servings

Fruit Sauce (Fruchtsoße)

        1¼ cup berries (raspberries, etc.)
        2   cups water
        1   tablespoon cornstarch
        1–2 tablespoons sugar

Wash and clean berries. In a pot, bring 2/3 cups water to a boil. Add berries, blend with a wire whisk, and cook over medium heat for about 5 minutes. In a cup, mix rest of water with cornstarch and sugar and carefully fold with fork into the berries. Simmer over low heat for about 10 minutes. If desired, add some more sugar.

Grandma's Tip: Use this sauce for puddings, oatmeal, fruits, or fruit purees.

Yield: 4 servings

Applesauce (Apfelsoße)

1   cup apple juice
½   tablespoon cornstarch
1   cup prepared applesauce
2   tablespoons raisins
1–2   tablespoons sugar (as desired)

In a pot, bring apple juice and cornstarch to a boil. Reduce heat and add applesauce, raisins, and sugar. Simmer over low heat for another 10 minutes.

Grandma's Tip: Use this sauce with puddings, pancakes, oatmeal, or just as a fruit dip.

Yield: 4 servings

Mocha Sauce (Mokkasoße)

2   cups milk
2   tablespoons sugar
1   teaspoon vanilla extract
dash salt
1   tablespoon cornstarch
½   cup strong coffee extract (2 tablespoons coffee grounds to ½ cup water)

In a pot, bring to a boil 1½ cups milk, sugar, vanilla extract, and salt. Remove from heat. Blend ½ cup milk with cornstarch and add to sugared milk. Quickly bring to a boil and simmer over low heat for about 5 minutes. Blend in the coffee extract.

Grandma's Tip: This sauce is used as a topping for puddings, ice cream, or fruit.

Yield: 4 servings

Chapter 7
Potatoes

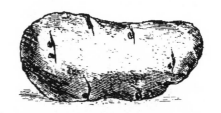

Chapter 7

Potatoes

Kartoffeln

Store potatoes in a dry, cold, well-ventilated room. Potatoes contain vitamin C, minerals, and proteins that are necessary for a balanced and healthy diet.

Mashed Potatoes (Kartoffelbrei)

5–7	potatoes
1	tablespoon butter
½	cup milk
1	teaspoon salt
1	teaspoon pepper
5	cups water
1	tablespoon salt

In a pot, bring water and salt to a boil. Add potatoes and cook until done. Strain potatoes and mash with a potato masher. Blend with a wire whisk or electric mixer. In a saucepan, heat milk and stir with butter, salt, and pepper into the potato mash.

Grandma's Tip: Serve with meat, fish, or poultry dishes. Top with gravy or, in skillet, fry 1 sliced onion in 2 tablespoons butter until golden and pour over mashed potatoes.

Yield: 4–5 servings

Buttered Parsley Potatoes (Petersiliekartoffeln)

6–8 potatoes
6 cups water
1 tablespoon and dash salt
2 tablespoons butter or margarine
3 tablespoons fresh parsley, finely chopped

Peel and cut potatoes into about 2-inch thick pieces. Rinse under cold water. In a pot, bring water with 1 tablespoon salt to a boil. Add potatoes. Cover and cook over medium heat until done. Strain water and fold potatoes together with butter, parsley, and salt.

Grandma's Tip: Serve parsley potatoes with meat, fish, or poultry dishes.

Yield: 4 servings

Potatoes in Different Sauces (Kartoffeln mit Verschiedenen Soßen)

For this recipe you can use either fresh, cooked, or leftover potatoes. Cut cooked potatoes into thin slices and simmer in desired sauce for about 8–10 minutes. Recommended sauces are: bechamel, bacon, onion, herb, anchovy, caraway, mustard, or mushroom sauce.

Potato Salad (Kartoffelsalat)

8–10	potatoes
5	dill pickle slices
1	cup hot beef broth
1	tablespoon vinegar
dash	salt
dash	sugar
dash	pepper
1	hard-boiled egg
2	tablespoons mayonnaise
1	small onion
1	tablespoon oil

In a large pot, with about 10 cups water and 1 tablespoon salt, cook potatoes until done. Peel and cut into slices. In a large bowl, mix beef broth with vinegar, salt, sugar, and pepper. Chop onion and pickles into small pieces. Combine with broth, sliced egg, potatoes, mayonnaise, and oil.

Grandma's Tip: Serve with sausages, bratwurst, German hamburgers, or other meat, fish, or poultry dishes. Garnish with sliced tomatoes and sprinkle with paprika and finely chopped fresh parsley, if desired.

Yield: 4–6 servings

Potato Salad with Cucumber
(Kartoffelsalat mit Gurken)

8–10	potatoes
dash	sugar
1	cucumber
1	onion
dash	salt
dash	pepper
½	cup beef broth
3	tablespoons mayonnaise
1	tablespoon vinegar
2	tablespoons finely chopped parsley and dill

In a large pot, with about 10 cups water and 1 tablespoon salt, boil potatoes until done. Peel and cut potatoes into slices. In a mixing bowl, finely shred peeled cucumber and combine with finely chopped onion, salt, pepper, sugar, vinegar, and broth. Carefully mix in potatoes, finely chopped parsley, dill, and mayonnaise.

Grandma's Tip: Serve this salad with bratwurst, sausages, German hamburgers, meat, fish, or poultry dishes. If desired, decorate with sliced tomato pieces, and sprinkle with paprika or finely chopped fresh parsley.

Yield: 4–6 servings

Hot Potato Salad (Warmer Kartoffelsalat)

8–10	potatoes
¼	pound bacon, finely chopped
1	small onion
1½	tablespoons flour
1	cup beef broth
1	tablespoon vinegar
dash	pepper
dash	sugar
dash	salt

In a large pot with about 10 cups water and 1 tablespoon salt, boil potatoes until done. Meanwhile in a saucepan, fry bacon with chopped onions until golden. Drain grease. Blend in the flour. Fill with beef broth and bring to a boil. Reduce heat and cook over medium heat for about 3 minutes. Combine with pepper, salt, vinegar, and sugar and stir. Peel potatoes, cut into thin slices, and carefully mix into the broth.

Grandma's Tip: Serve with bratwurst, German hamburgers, fried fish, or meat dishes.

Yield: 4–6 servings

Potato Ragout (*Kartoffelragout*)

6	potatoes
1	small finely chopped onion
1	bell pepper, finely sliced
3	tablespoons margarine or butter
dash	salt
1	tablespoon flour
1	tablespoon tomato paste
2	cups beef or chicken broth
4	slices sweet and sour or dill pickles
dash	pepper
dash	paprika
1	clove garlic, minced

Peel potatoes, cut into small cubes or slices. In a pot, melt margarine. Brown onions, bell pepper, and potato slices in butter. Blend in pepper, salt, paprika, and minced garlic. Sprinkle with flour. Stir in the broth. Bring to a boil. Reduce heat and cook over medium heat for about 20 minutes. Blend in tomato paste and sliced pickles.

Grandma's Tip: Sprinkle with finely chopped parsley. For better digestion, add 1 tablespoon caraway seeds. Serve with bratwurst, sausages, or fried fish.

Yield: 4 servings

Creamed Potatoes *(Kartoffeln in Heller Soße)*

6	potatoes
dash	salt
2/3	cup milk
2/3	cup liquid whipping cream
2	tablespoons butter
½	cup shredded cheese (cheddar or mozzarella)
½	tablespoon cornstarch

Preheat oven to 350 degrees. Peel potatoes and cut into thin slices. Sprinkle with salt and put into greased casserole dish. In a bowl, blend milk, whipping cream, and cornstarch. Pour over potatoes. Cover dish and put into the preheated oven for about 20 minutes or until potatoes are cooked. Take out of the oven. Remove the cover and sprinkle with butter flakes and cheese. Return to the oven and bake for another 5 minutes or until cheese is melted.

Grandma's Tip: If desired, add fresh herbs such as basil, marjoram, fresh parsley, dill, or chives. Serve with fish, meat, or poultry dishes.

Yield: 4 servings

Potato and Egg Casserole *(Kartoffel-Eier-Auflauf)*

6–8	cooked potatoes
1	cup sour cream
4	hard boiled eggs
3	tablespoons finely chopped parsley
4	medium-sized tomatoes
2	onions
5	tablespoons margarine or butter
1	cup milk
dash	salt

Peel cooked potatoes and boiled eggs. Cut potatoes, eggs, and tomatoes into slices. In a pot, melt 2 tablespoons margarine. Add sliced onions and brown until golden. In a casserole dish, make alternating layers of potatoes, eggs, and tomatoes. Sprinkle browned onions and parsley between layers. In a bowl, blend sour cream with milk and salt. Pour over the potatoes. Dab the rest of the butter on top of potatoes. Bake in a preheated 320 degree oven for about 45 minutes.

Grandma's Tip: Sprinkle with shredded mozzarella or cheddar cheese. Put back into the oven and bake again until cheese is melted and browned.

Yield: 4–5 servings

Potato Pieces with Vegetables *(Kartoffeln mit Gemüse)*

1½	cups finely chopped vegetables (carrots, cabbage, celery root, as desired)
8	potatoes
dash	salt
2	tablespoons margarine
1	cup water
4	cups beef broth
1	tablespoon chopped parsley
dash	pepper
1½	tablespoons flour

Clean and chop vegetables. In a pot, bring water and vegetables to a boil. Add margarine and salt. Cook over medium heat for about 10 minutes. In a pot, bring beef broth to a boil. Add peeled and cut potatoes and cook over medium heat until done. Blend 3 tablespoons water with the flour and stir into potatoes. Strain vegetables and add to potatoes. Sprinkle with salt, pepper, and parsley and stir.

Grandma's Tip: If desired, add 2 cloves minced garlic and 1 tablespoon caraway seeds. Serve with meat, fish, poultry dishes, bratwurst, sausages, or German hamburgers.

Yield: 4 servings

Potato Souffle with Bratwurst
(Kartoffel-Souffle mit Bratwurst)

4	bratwurst
1	tablespoon flour
4	tablespoons margarine or butter
6–8	potatoes
1	cup beef broth
1	cup sour cream
2	tablespoons chopped parsley
1	medium onion
2	green onions
1	teaspoon salt

Sprinkle bratwurst with flour and brown in a skillet with 2 tablespoons melted margarine or butter until golden on all sides. Peel and cut potatoes into slices. In a pot, melt 2 tablespoons margarine or butter. Cut bratwurst into 1 or 1½ inch cubes. Place in the pot and cover with sliced onions. Sprinkle with salt and add the broth. In a bowl, blend sour cream with flour and fold with the sliced potatoes into the broth. Cover and cook over medium heat for about 45 minutes. Fold in chopped green onion and finely chopped parsley.

Grandma's Tip: Serve this dish with fresh garden salad or lettuce in oil and vinegar dressing. You could also prepare this dish in a baking dish in a 350 degree preheated oven. Bake for about 45 minutes to 1 hour.

Yield: 4 servings

Potato Dumplings (Kartoffelklöße)

4	cups water with ½ tablespoon salt
8	cups water with 1 tablespoon salt
6	potatoes
1/3	cup flour
½	cup cornstarch
1	egg
dash	salt
dash	nutmeg
1	slice toast
2	tablespoons butter

In a pot, bring 4 cups water and salt to a boil. Add peeled potatoes and cook over medium heat until done. Strain water. Put potatoes in a large bowl, and mash with a potato masher. With a fork blend in the flour, cornstarch, eggs, salt, and nutmeg. In a large pot, bring 8 cups water with salt to a boil. In a skillet, melt butter. Add ½ inch thick toast cubes and brown until golden. Wet hands under cold water. With a large spoon, scoop dough into your hands. Make a well and add 1 to 2 cubes of browned toast and form round dumpling balls around the toast. With a spatula or large spoon, dip dumplings into the boiling water. Reduce heat and cook over medium heat for about 20 minutes. Remove dumplings with a spatula so water will strain.

Grandma's Tip: Dumplings are usually recognized as done once they start coming up to the surface of the water. If you use leftover dumplings the next day, cut them into ½ inch slices and fry in skillet with butter at both sides until golden. Serve dumplings with roasts, meat loaf in gravy, vegetables, and a salad. For richer dumplings, add 2 tablespoons cream cheese to the batter, fill with chopped onions, or fold fresh parsley into the batter.

Yield: 4 servings

Thueringer Potato Dumpling (Thüringer Kartoffelklöße)

9	potatoes
dash	salt
½	cup milk
2	slices wheat or white bread
1	tablespoon butter or margarine
8–10	cups water with 1½ tablespoons salt
3	cups water with ½ tablespoon salt

Peel and wash potatoes. Finely grate 6 potatoes with a grater. In a saucepan, bring 3 cups salt water to a boil, add 3 potatoes and cook until done. Place grated potatoes in a clean kitchen linen towel. Squeeze and extract as much liquid as possible. Dry grated potatoes again with 3 or 4 layers of paper towels. Crumble up dry potatoes and sprinkle with salt. Strain water from cooked potatoes. Put back into the saucepan. Add milk and mash with a potato masher. Pour the crumbled potatoes over the mashed potatoes. Mix together in a pot. Over medium heat, stir potato dough until it turns into a sticky dough that easily loosens from the sides of the pot. In a skillet, melt butter or margarine. Cut bread into cubes and brown until golden. In a pot, bring 8–10 cups salt water to a boil. Wet hands under cold water. Scoop dumpling batter into your hands with a large spoon. Make a well and fill with 2–3 bread cubes. Form round dumpling balls and place in the boiling water with a large spoon or spatula. Reduce heat and cook over medium heat for about 20 minutes. Remove dumplings with a spatula so water will drain.

Grandma's Tip: Extract as much liquid as possible from grated potatoes. Serve with meat or poultry dishes with gravy. Slice leftover dumplings into 1 inch thick slices and fry them in oil or butter on both sides until golden.

Yield: 4 servings

Raised Sweet Dumplings (Hefeklösse)

8–10	cups water with 1 tablespoon salt
2¼	cups flour
1	cup milk
¼	ounce (1 package) yeast
1	teaspoon salt
½	cups sugar
5	ounces or 2/3 cup margarine
2	eggs
dash	salt

Sift the flour into a large bowl and sprinkle with salt. In a saucepan, heat the milk until lukewarm. Blend sugar, eggs, yeast, and melted margarine into the flour. Stir everything together until you have a smooth dough. Sprinkle with about 2 tablespoons flour. Cover with a clean linen kitchen towel and set aside for about 1 hour or until dough rises. Dip hands into flour and knead dough again. Form round dumpling balls. Roll dumplings on a floured cutting board and set aside for another 10 minutes. In a large pot with a steamer insert, bring salt water to a boil. Place dumplings in steamer, cover with a lid or bowl and simmer over the steam for about 15 minutes. Set aside for 5 minutes and serve.

Grandma's Tip: If you do not have a steamer insert, tie a clean linen kitchen towel tightly over the pot with a string and set dumplings on top of that. To ensure good rising of dough, put dry yeast in ¼ of the milk (warmed) and set aside before adding to dough. Serve dumplings with a sweet sauce, like pear sauce.

Pear Sauce: In a pot, bring to a boil 1 can pears with juice and ¼ water. Blend in 1 tablespoon flour. Reduce heat and stir. For a larger recipe, use 2 cans pears with ½ cup water and 2 tablespoons cornstarch. Blend in 2–3 tablespoons raisins and 1 teaspoon clove powder, if desired.

Yield: 4–6 servings

Dumpling Noodles (Kartoffelnudeln)

1 recipe potato dumpling dough made with cooked potatoes
1 cup cornstarch
8 cups water
½ tablespoon salt
¼ cup bread crumbs
½ cup oil

Cut dough into 10 pieces. Separate each into four parts. Form dough into finger length rolls and toss in cornstarch. In a large pot, bring water and salt to a boil, and add the dumpling noodles. Cook over medium heat for about 15 minutes. Strain water, carefully pat noddles dry with a paper towel, and toss in bread crumbs. Heat the oil in a large skillet. Add noodles and brown until golden. Remove with a spatula and pat dry.

Grandma's Tip: Sprinkle with salt and pepper. Serve with meat dishes or use as snack with ketchup-mayonnaise dip.

Yield: 4–6 servings

Plum Dumplings (Klöße mit Pflaumen)

8–10 cups water with 1 tablespoon salt
1 recipe dumpling dough (made with cooked potatoes) or raised sweet dumpling dough
2 tablespoons sugar
7 whole fresh plums
7 cubes sugar
3 tablespoons butter
2 tablespoons cinnamon sugar

Form about 7 dumplings out of the dough and make a well in the corner of each. Remove pits from plums and fill with a sugar cube. Place the plum into the well of the dough. Wet hands with cold water and form dough into round dumplings. In a large pot, bring water to a boil. With a large spoon, gently place dumplings into the water. Reduce heat and cook over medium heat for about 20 minutes. Pour melted butter over the dumplings and sprinkle with cinnamon sugar.

Grandma's Tip: Serve dumplings with hot vanilla sauce. Dumplings are done when they rise to the surface of the water.

Yield: 4 servings

Dumplings with Bacon (Klöße mit Speck)

1   recipe dumpling dough (made with cooked potatoes)
7   slices bacon
8   cups salt water

Prepare dumpling dough and, in a skillet, fry bacon until golden. Pat bacon dry with a paper towel to remove the excess fat. Wet hands with cold water. Scoop dumpling dough into your hand. Make a well in the center and place 1 slice bacon in each dumpling. In a large pot, bring salt water to a boil. Gently place dumplings in water and cook over medium heat for about 20 minutes.

Grandma's Tip: Instead of using whole bacon slices, dice bacon into small pieces and saute with onion slices. Dumplings are done when they rise to the surface of the water.

Yield: 4 servings

Potato Balls (Kartoffelbällchen)

½   batch of dumpling dough (made with cooked potatoes)
½   cup oil
1   egg, lightly beaten
½   cup bread crumbs

Make half a recipe of dumpling dough. Form small balls. Roll in the egg and then in the bread crumbs. In a large skillet, heat the oil and fry dumplings in the oil until golden brown. Pat dry with a paper towel.

Grandma's Tip: For variety, add fresh herbs (finely chopped parsley, chives, basil, etc.) to the dough. Serve with fish or meat dishes or just use it as a snack with a ketchup and mayonnaise marinade. (Blend 5 tablespoons ketchup with 2 tablespoons mayonnaise.)

Yield: 4 servings

French Fries (Pommes Frites)

5   potatoes
2   cups oil
dash   salt

Peel potatoes and cut into small strips. Rinse in a strainer and pat dry with a paper towel. In a large skillet, heat the oil and add potato strips. Fry over medium heat until golden brown and tender. Continually turn with a spatula.

Grandma's Tip: Pat dry with paper towel to remove excess oil. Serve with mayonnaise-ketchup marinade. (Mix 5 tablespoons ketchup with 2 tablespoons mayonnaise)

Yield: 3–4 servings

Fried Potatoes (Bratkartoffeln)

- 5–6 potatoes
- ½ cup oil
- 1 sliced onion
- 2 teaspoons salt
- 2 teaspoons pepper
- 2 teaspoons paprika
- 1 tablespoon caraway seeds
- 2 tablespoons finely chopped parsley and chives

Peel and cut potatoes into slices. Heat the oil in a large skillet. Add potato slices. Sprinkle with salt, pepper, paprika and onion. Fry over medium heat for about 20 minutes. Continually turn with a spatula. Sprinkle with caraway seeds and cook again for another 10 minutes or until potatoes are tender. Sprinkle with finely chopped parsley and chives.

Grandma's Tip: Serve potatoes with bratwurst, sausages, German hamburgers, vegetables, fresh lettuce, or a garden salad.

Yield: 4 servings

Potato Chips (Kartoffelchips)

- 5 potatoes
- 2 cups oil
- salt

Cut washed and peeled potatoes into very thin slices and soak for about 10 minutes in cold water. Heat the oil in a large skillet. Add potato slices and cook over medium heat for about 3–5 minutes or until light golden brown. With a spatula, remove chips from oil, set on a paper towel, and sprinkle with salt.

Grandma's Tip: You also could sprinkle chips with a dash of paprika. Serve with cold fondue sauce or dip.

Yield: 4 servings

Ravioli Dumplings (Ravioli Klößchen)

6–8	cooked potatoes
½	cup flour
¼	cup cornstarch
dash	salt
dash	nutmeg
4	tablespoons margarine
1	egg, slightly beaten
2	tablespoons bread crumbs
½	cup oil

Mash cooked potatoes with a potato masher and combine with cornstarch, flour, salt, nutmeg, 2 tablespoons margarine, and the egg. Knead into a dough. Roll dough into a ½ inch thick layer and spread 2 tablespoon margarine evenly on top. Sprinkle dough with bread crumbs, cut into 2 inch slices, and roll up slices, gently squeezing together. In a large skillet, heat the oil and fry ravioli on both sides until golden, or bake on a greased baking sheet in a 350 degree oven for about 20 minutes.

Grandma's Tip: Sprinkle dough with additional flour to make it easier to roll. For variety, spread with tomato paste and chopped onions or seasoned hamburger meat.

Yield: 4 servings

Potato Pancakes (Kartoffelküchle)

    6   potatoes
    ½   cup flour
 dash   salt
    ½   cup oil
    ½   finely chopped onion
    ½   grated onion
    1   egg, lightly beaten

Peel and grate potatoes with a grater. Add the flour, egg, and finely chopped onion. Sprinkle with salt. With a fork, blend everything together until the dough is smooth. Add grated onion and stir again. In a skillet, heat the oil. Add about 1 ladle full of dough and fry pancakes over medium heat on both sides until golden.

Grandma's Tip: Pat pancakes dry with paper towel to remove excess oil. Serve immediately so they will be fresh. To keep pancakes warm, put them on a baking sheet and set in preheated 200 degree oven. Serve with applesauce or a fresh garden salad.

Yield: 4 servings

Chapter 8
Breakfast
Foods

Chapter 8

Breakfast Foods

Frühstück

Creamed Omelette (Kremomelett)

3	eggs, separated
dash	salt
½	tablespoon cornstarch
1/3	cup oil
dash	pepper

In a bowl, beat the egg yolks until creamy and sprinkle with a dash of salt and pepper. In a separate bowl, beat egg whites until stiff and carefully fold with the cornstarch into the creamed egg yolks. Heat the oil in a skillet. Add the batter and brown the bottom until golden. Slide omelette onto a preheated plate. Top with desired filling and fold in half.

Yield: 2 servings

Sweet Filled Omelette (Süße gefüllte Omeletts)

        1   recipe creamed omelette
    1/3   cup sugar
        1   tablespoon lemon juice
        1   tablespoon lemon peel
      ½   tablespoon cornstarch

Blend ingredients into the creamed omelette batter. Spread omelette with a whole fruit jam or fill with stewed fruit.

Grandma's Tip: To finish the omelette, cover skillet for the last few minutes or prepare omelette on baking sheet in a preheated 350 degree oven.

Mushroom Omelette (Pilzomeletts)

        1   recipe omelette batter
      ½   cup fresh or canned, diced mushrooms
  dash   salt
  dash   pepper
        1   diced tomato
        2   lettuce leaves
        1   tablespoon margarine
      ½   onion, chopped

In a skillet, melt margarine and brown onion with mushrooms until golden. Sprinkle with salt and pepper. Add diced tomato. Stir everything together and cook over medium heat for about 5 minutes. Fold chopped lettuce leaves into the omelette.

Grandma's Tip: Make sure mushrooms are hot when adding to eggs. Sprinkle with fresh chopped parsley and chives.

Sausage Links *(Omelett mit Würstchen)*

1	recipe omelette batter
¼	pound hot sausage cubes
3	ounces Philadelphia cream cheese
8	ounces Velveeta cheese
½	chopped onion
dash	salt
dash	pepper
1	tablespoon margarine

In a skillet, melt margarine and brown hot sausage cubes with onion until golden. Strain grease, reduce heat, and slowly blend in the cheese. Sprinkle with salt and pepper and fold into the omelette.

Strawberry Filling for Sweet Omelette *(Erdbeeromelett)*

1	package frozen strawberries
1	tablespoon sugar
½	tablespoon cornstarch
½	tablespoon lemon juice
1	tablespoon lemon peel

In a large saucepan, simmer strawberries over low heat until defrosted. Remove about 2 tablespoons liquid and blend with cornstarch. Bring strawberries to a quick boil and fold in cornstarch mixture. Stir in sugar, lemon juice, and lemon peel.

Grandma's Tip: To refine, sprinkle with almonds or chopped nuts.

Pancakes (Pfannekuchen)

1	cup milk
dash	salt
2/3	cup flour
2	eggs
dash	sugar
½	cup oil

In a bowl, blend eggs, milk, flour, salt, and sugar together. In a skillet, heat the oil and pour about 1 ladle full of batter into the pan. Over medium heat, brown pancakes on both sides until golden.

Grandma's Tip: To remove excess grease, pat pancakes dry with a paper towel. Sprinkle with sugar or spread with whole fruit jam. Instead of sugar, try adding a dash of pepper to the batter and top with either fried mushrooms, ham, or bacon.

Yield: 3 servings

Pancakes with Sliced Apples (Pfannekuchen mit Äpfel)

2	eggs
1	cup milk
2/3	cup flour
dash	salt and sugar
2	apples
½	cup oil
2	tablespoons cinnamon sugar

In a bowl, blend the eggs, milk, flour, salt, and sugar together. Heat the oil in a skillet. Pour about 1 ladle full of pancake batter into the oil. Layer with 3–4 thinly sliced apple pieces and sprinkle with cinnamon sugar.

Grandma's Tip: To decrease fat, pat dry with paper towels. Sprinkle with chopped almonds or nuts, if desired.

Yield: 3 servings

Pancakes with Bacon (Pfannekuchen mit Speck)

2	eggs
2/3	cup milk
2/3	cup flour
dash	salt
dash	pepper
½	chopped onion
¼	pound bacon
½	cup oil
1	tablespoon margarine

In a bowl, blend the eggs, milk, flour, salt, and pepper together. In a skillet, melt margarine. Add chopped bacon cubes and onion. Brown bacon and drain the grease. In a separate skillet, heat the oil and pour about 1 ladle full of pancake batter into the pan. Layer each with one part of fried bacon and onion. After one side is browned, carefully flip over with a spatula and brown the other side.

Grandma's Tip: To remove excess fat, pat dry with a paper towel. Pancakes with bacon are good served with freshly prepared lettuce with sour cream-herbal dressing. Just top pancakes with the salad.

Austrian Pancakes with Raisins
(Kaiserschmarrn)

4	eggs, separated
½	cup oil
¼	cup raisins
1	cup milk
4	tablespoons sugar
1	teaspoon vanilla or almond extract
1½	tablespoons rum or 1 tablespoon rum extract mixed with ½ tablespoon water
2	tablespoons chopped almonds
3	tablespoons powdered sugar
1–3/4	cups flour

Drizzle raisins with rum or rum extract. Mix and set aside for about 1 hour. In a bowl, blend the egg yolks with sugar, flour, milk, raisins, vanilla or almond extract. Blend the egg whites with an electric mixer until stiff. Fold into the egg batter. In a skillet, heat the oil and scoop about 1½ ladles of batter into the hot oil. Sprinkle with almonds and brown both sides for a few minutes until golden. If desired, cut into slices and sprinkle with powdered sugar.

Grandma's Tip: Pat pancakes dry with paper towel to remove excess oil. Instead of using rum-soaked raisins, try plain raisins. You can also bake apple slices into the batter.

Yield: 4 servings

Cream Cheese Dumplings (Käsesahneklöße)

2	eggs
3/4	cup flour
¼	cup cornstarch
dash	salt
½	cup sugar
16	ounces cream cheese
2	tablespoons raisins
1	teaspoon lemon peel
7–9	cups water with salt

In a bowl, blend eggs with sugar and mix with cream cheese, flour, and cornstarch. Fold in raisins, lemon peel, and salt. In a large pot, bring water to a boil. Dip hands into flour, form round dumpling balls, and drop into the boiling water. Reduce heat and cook dumplings over medium heat for about 15 minutes.

Grandma's Tip: If dough is too sticky, add some more flour. Do not forget to sprinkle your hands with flour or it will be difficult to form dumplings. Serve dumplings with sweet vanilla, chocolate, or almond sauce.

Yield: 4–5 servings

Cream Cheese Pancakes (Käsesahne Pfannekuchen)

14	ounces cream cheese
2/3	cup milk
½	cup flour
½	cup cornstarch
1	teaspoon baking powder
2	eggs
dash	salt
dash	pepper
½	finely chopped onion
1	clove garlic, finely minced
1	tablespoon finely chopped chives
1	tablespoon finely chopped parsley
½	cup oil

In a bowl, blend eggs, cream cheese, and milk. Fold in the baking powder, flour, and cornstarch. Stir in chopped onion, garlic, chives, and parsley. Sprinkle with salt and pepper. In a large skillet, heat the oil, pour about 1 ladle full of batter into the hot oil. Reduce heat and brown both sides over medium heat until golden brown.

Grandma's Tip: For variety, fold about 1 tablespoon caraway seeds into the batter. Serve with a fresh garden salad.

Yield: 4 servings

Cream Cheese Casserole (Käsesahne Auflauf)

        1½   pounds cream cheese
         3   eggs, separated
        1½   cups milk
        3/4 cup sugar
         2   teaspoons vanilla extract
         2   tablespoons butter or margarine
         2   tablespoons raisins
         1   tablespoon grated lemon peel
         1   cup strained cherries
         3   tablespoons cornstarch
      dash   salt

In a bowl, beat the egg yolks. Add milk, cream cheese, cornstarch, vanilla extract, sugar, and lemon peel. Mix everything together. In a separate bowl, beat the egg whites until stiff. Sprinkle with a dash of salt and fold into the cream cheese batter. Blend in raisins and cherries. Fill a greased baking dish, top with butter flakes, place in a preheated 320 degree oven, and bake for about 40–50 minutes.

Grandma's Tip: For easier removal after baking, sprinkle baking dish with about 3 tablespoons bread crumbs. As a variation, sprinkle with chopped almonds or add sliced apples to the cream cheese batter.

Yield: 5 servings

Chapter 9

Vegetables

Chapter 9

Vegetables

Gemüse

Vegetables are very high in vitamins, minerals, and trace elements. Store vegetables in a cool and dark place. The fresher you use vegetables, the more vitamins and minerals they contain. Wash and clean vegetables very well before processing, but never leave vegetables in water for a long time. The vitamin and mineral content is reduced if you prepare vegetables in a copper, zinc, or enamelware dish. Never boil vegetables on high; always use medium heat or just simmer. Only use a small amount of water to cook vegetables unless you are processing certain vegetables (such as asparagus, cauliflower, or vegetables cooked in soup). Never fully cook vegetables in order to minimize loss of vitamins. Use the vegetable broth later in the food preparation process, since a part of the minerals and vitamins are transferring into the water.

Carrot Vegetables (Karottengemüse)

1–3/4	pounds fresh carrots
2	tablespoons margarine
2	cups water
1	tablespoon chopped parsley
dash	salt
dash	pepper

Wash, clean, and peel carrots. Cut into ½ inch slices. In a pot, bring water, 1 tablespoon margarine, and salt to a boil. Add carrots and cover. Cook over medium heat for about 20 minutes or until the carrots are tender. Strain water, fold in 1 tablespoon margarine, and sprinkle with pepper, salt, and finely chopped parsley.

Grandma's Tip: Serve with potatoes and a meat dish. Try serving carrots in a light buttered gravy. In a saucepan, melt 1 tablespoon margarine. Brown ½ chopped onion. Blend 1 cup water with 1 tablespoon flour and stir into the browned onions. Fold in the strained carrots.

Yield: 4 servings

Carrot Casserole (Karottenauflauf)

1½	pounds fresh carrots
3	potatoes
1	small onion, finely chopped
4	tablespoons margarine or butter
2	tablespoons shredded mozzarella cheese
1	tablespoon flour
1	cup beef broth
1	cup milk
dash	salt
dash	paprika
1	egg, separated

Clean, peel, and cut carrots and potatoes into ½-inch thick slices. In a pot, melt 1 tablespoon margarine or butter and brown the onion. Sprinkle with flour and stir until flour turns light golden brown. Slowly stir in milk and broth.

Season with paprika and salt. Grease a baking dish with 1 tablespoon margarine or butter and layer potatoes and carrots. Blend the egg yolk into the broth and stir rapidly. In a bowl, beat the egg white until stiff and then fold into the broth. Pour over layered carrots and potatoes. Top casserole with 2 tablespoons margarine or butter flakes and shredded cheese or bake in a preheated 320 degree oven for about 40 minutes.

Grandma's Tip: To give the casserole a fresh taste, fold in 2 tablespoons finely chopped fresh parsley or chives. Serve with German hamburgers, sausage, bratwurst, or pork chops.

Yield: 4 servings

Glazed Carrots (Glasierte Karotten)

1½	pounds fresh carrots
2	tablespoons sugar
dash	salt
2	tablespoons margarine
1	tablespoon chopped parsley
1	tablespoon chopped dill
2/3	cup water
dash	pepper

In a pot, brown the sugar until light golden. Add cleaned and sliced carrots (or whole baby carrots). In a saucepan, bring water to a boil and blend into the carrots. Sprinkle with salt and pepper. Blend in margarine. Cover and cook over medium heat for 20–30 minutes or until carrots are tender. Sprinkle with finely chopped herbs.

Grandma's Tip: Serve glazed carrots with parsley potatoes, boiled potatoes, German hamburgers, sausages, bratwurst, or pork chops. If desired, add ½ finely chopped onion.

Yield: 4 servings

Carrot Casserole with Meat
(Karottenauflauf mit Fleisch)

1	pound beef or pork stew meat
7	cups water
1	medium onion
dash	salt
3–4	bay leaf
4	potatoes
1¼	pounds carrots
1	tablespoon chopped chives
1	tablespoon flour
3	tablespoons finely chopped parsley

In a large pot, with about 3 cups water, add chopped meat, chopped onion, salt, and bay leaves. Reduce heat and cook over medium heat for about 30 minutes. Cut potatoes and carrots into 3/4-inch cubes. Add to the meat and fill with 4 more cups of water. Cover and cook over medium heat for another 30 minutes. Stir occasionally. Blend flour with 3 tablespoons water and stir into the stew. Before serving, sprinkle with finely chopped parsley and chives.

Grandma's Tip: For more flavor, add 2 cloves finely minced garlic and cook 3–5 peppercorns with the meat.

Yield: 4–5 servings

Carrot and Bean Stew (Karotten-Bohnen Stew)

1	pound beef or pork stew meat
2	tablespoons flour
1	onion
7½	cups water
½	pound fresh green beans
1¼	pounds carrots
dash	salt
1	teaspoon marjoram
2	potatoes
2	bay leaves
1	teaspoon pepper
2	tablespoons finely chopped parsley

In a large pot, bring 7½ cups water to a boil. Add chopped meat, salt, pepper, chopped onion, and bay leaves. Cook over medium heat for about 30 minutes. Add cleaned and chopped carrots, beans, and potato pieces. Cover and cook over medium heat for another 20–30 minutes. Sprinkle with marjoram. Blend ½ cup water with the flour. Bring stew to a boil and fold the flour into the stew. Remove about 2 ladles full of stew. Mash with a potato masher and return to the pot. Cook over medium heat again for another 15–20 minutes. Stir once in a while. Before serving, sprinkle with finely chopped parsley.

Grandma's Tip: Instead of beef or pork stew, try using smoked ham, pork or beef ribs. Serve with boiled potatoes.

Yield: 4–5 servings

Baked Asparagus (Gebackener Spargel)

1-3/4	pounds fresh asparagus, washed and peeled
4	cups water
dash	salt
1	teaspoon sugar
4	tablespoons butter
1	cup shredded mozzarella cheese

In a pot, bring water to a boil. Add asparagus, sprinkle with salt and sugar, and cook over medium heat for about 20 minutes or until asparagus is tender. Strain the water. Pat asparagus dry with a paper towel and place in a greased stoneware casserole or baking dish. Top with butter flakes and shredded cheese. Bake in a 350 degree preheated oven for about 10–15 minutes or until cheese melts and turns golden brown.

Grandma's Tip: Serve with breaded pork chops, German hamburgers, meat, or chicken dishes.

Yield: 4 servings

Celery Roots (Selleriegemüse)

       2   large celery roots
       2   tablespoons margarine or butter
     2/3   cup water
       1   medium chopped onion
       1   recipe hollandaise sauce
       1   tablespoon chopped chives
    dash   salt
       2   tablespoons finely chopped parsley

Peel celery roots and chop into cubes. In a large saucepan, bring water and margarine or butter to a boil. Add celery roots, onion, and salt. Cook over medium heat for about 20 minutes. Stir occasionally. Drain water and fold in hollandaise sauce. Sprinkle with finely chopped parsley and chives.

Grandma's Tip: Serve with a meat dish without gravy, such as German hamburgers, sausages, bratwurst, or pork chops. If served with a meat dish and gravy, do not use hollandaise sauce. Instead, just combine with 2 tablespoons butter and sprinkle with salt.

Yield: 3–4 servings

Asparagus Vegetable (Spargelgemüse)

   1–3/4   pounds fresh asparagus, washed and peeled
       2   cups water
    dash   salt
       1   teaspoon sugar
       3   tablespoons butter
       1   tablespoon flour
       1   egg yolk
       1   teaspoon lemon juice

Cut asparagus into 1-inch pieces. In a pot, bring water to a boil. Add asparagus, sugar, salt, and 1 tablespoon butter. Cook over medium heat for about 20 minutes. In a separate pot, melt 2 tablespoons butter. Stir in the flour and fold in the hot asparagus mixture. Carefully stir, quickly bring to a boil and remove from heat. Blend in the egg yolk and drizzle with lemon juice.

Grandma's Tip: You also can serve asparagus with hollandaise sauce. If you do, strain water and blend into hollandaise sauce. Serve with meat or chicken dishes without gravy such as breaded pork chops, German hamburgers, or bratwurst.

Yield: 4 servings

------- ⊷•••⦅⦆••⊶ -------

Kohlrabi (Kohlrabigemüse)

2	pounds fresh kohlrabi
1½	cups plus 2 tablespoons water
dash	salt
3	tablespoons margarine
1	tablespoon finely chopped parsley
1	teaspoon flour

Wash, peel, and chop kohlrabi into pieces. In a pot, bring water, salt, and margarine to a boil. Add kohlrabi and cover. Cook over medium heat for about 15 minutes or until the kohlrabi is tender. In a cup, blend flour with water and stir into the boiling kohlrabi. Reduce heat, cook over medium heat for another 5 minutes, and sprinkle with parsley.

Grandma's Tip: Kohlrabi can also be served with hollandaise sauce. Strain the water and fold together with the sauce. Serve with breaded pork chops, German hamburgers, sausages, or bratwurst and boiled potatoes.

Yield: 3–4 servings

------- ⊷•••⦅⦆••⊶ -------

Leeks (Lauchgemüse)

```
7–8   stalks fresh leeks
   2   cups plus 3 tablespoons water
dash   salt
   2   tablespoons margarine
   1   tablespoon flour
dash   paprika
   1   medium onion
   1   tablespoon caraway seeds
   2   tablespoons finely chopped parsley
```

Cut leaves of leeks in stages so it will be easier to remove dirt. Cut leeks into 1-inch slices. In a pot, bring water to a boil. Add leeks and chopped onion. Cook over medium heat for about 20 minutes. In a skillet, melt margarine, add flour, and blend in 3 tablespoons water. Bring leeks to a boil, stir in the flour mixture. Sprinkle with salt, paprika, and caraway seeds. Cook over medium heat for another 10 minutes. Before serving, sprinkle with finely chopped parsley.

Grandma's Tip: Serve leeks with boiled or parsley potatoes, German hamburgers, breaded pork chops, sausages, or bratwurst.

Yield: 4 servings

Fennel (Fenchelgemüse)

```
  1½   pounds fresh fennel
1–2/3   cups vegetable or beef broth
   2   tablespoons margarine or butter
   1   tablespoon flour
dash   salt
dash   paprika
   1   tablespoon finely chopped parsley
```

Wash and peel fennel. Remove roots from the vegetable and cut in quarters or slices. In a pot, bring broth to a boil. Add fennel pieces and cook over medium heat for about 20 minutes. In a large saucepan, melt margarine and blend with flour. Strain broth from fennel and blend into the flour. Add fennel and simmer over low heat for another 10 minutes. Sprinkle with salt, paprika, and finely chopped parsley.

Grandma's Tip: To refine, blend in 1 tablespoon tomato paste. Serve with boiled or parsley potatoes, bratwurst, sausages, German hamburgers, or breaded pork chops.

Yield: 3 servings

Stewed Onions (Zwiebelgemüse)

1	pound onions
3	fresh tomatoes or 2 green bell peppers
3	tablespoons margarine
1	tablespoon flour
3	tablespoons sour cream
¼	cup beef broth
1	teaspoon salt
1	teaspoon pepper
1	teaspoon sugar
½–1	tablespoon caraway seeds
4	cups water

Peel and slice onions into pieces. In a saucepan, bring water to a boil and dip tomatoes into the water for about 2–3 minutes. Remove tomatoes from water. Peel and slice them. In a saucepan, melt margarine. Add tomatoes or cleaned bell pepper slices and sliced onions. Stir and cook over medium heat for about 10 minutes or until light golden brown. In a bowl, blend flour with broth and sour cream and stir into the hot vegetables. Simmer for another 5 minutes. Sprinkle with salt, pepper, sugar, and caraway seeds.

Grandma's Tip: To reduce the calories, use ½ cup beef broth instead of sour cream.

Glazed Onions (Glasierte Zwiebeln)

4–5 small onions
  3 tablespoons margarine
  2 tablespoons oil
  1 tablespoon sugar

Peel and cut onions into slices. In a skillet, heat the oil and margarine. Add onions, sprinkle with sugar, and cook over medium heat until golden brown. Stir continually.

Grandma's Tip: If desired, sprinkle with 1–2 tablespoons finely chopped parsley and ½ tablespoon caraway seeds. Serve with pork chops, bratwurst, or steaks, and boiled potatoes.

Yield: 3–4 servings

Chicory (Chicorygemüse)

4–5 chicory sticks
  2 tablespoons margarine
  1 cup water
  1 teaspoon salt
  1 recipe hollandaise sauce

Wash and clean chicory. Remove all wilted leaves, cut into slices or cubes, and pat dry with a paper towel. Meanwhile, in a large saucepan, bring water, salt, and margarine to a boil. Add chicory. Cover and cook over medium heat for about 15–20 minutes. Strain water and top with the hollandaise sauce.

Grandma's Tip: Chicory can also be served raw as a salad. Rinse under water, cut into slices, and blend with a vinegar and oil salad dressing. Serve cooked chicory with boiled potatoes, pork chops, German hamburgers, sausages, or bratwurst.

Yield: 4 servings

Baked Chicory (Gebackener Chicory)

4	sticks chicory
1	cup water
1	teaspoon salt
4	slices ham
½	cup shredded cheese
3	tablespoons margarine or butter
2	tablespoons tomato paste or ketchup

In a pot, bring salt water to a boil. Add washed and cleaned chicory sticks. Remove all wilted leaves and add to the water. Cook over medium heat for about 3–5 minutes. Strain water and pat vegetables dry with a paper towel. Spread tomato paste or ketchup on the ham and wrap around the chicory. Tighten with a toothpick. Spread with margarine or butter and sprinkle with cheese. Set chicories into a greased casserole or baking dish and bake in a preheated 350 degree oven for about 10 minutes or until cheese is light golden brown and melted.

Grandma's Tip: If you do not have toothpicks handy, tighten chicory rolls with thread. Baked chicory can be served with hollandaise sauce, boiled potatoes, bratwurst, German hamburgers, or pork chops.

Yield: 4 servings

Cabbage (Krautgemüse)

1-3/4 pounds cabbage
1 tablespoon finely chopped parsley
1 teaspoon caraway seeds
1 cup beef broth
2 tablespoons margarine
1 tablespoon oil
1 onion
½ tablespoon salt

Wash and cut cabbage into slices. In a pot, bring broth, oil, and margarine to a boil. Add the cabbage and chopped onion. Sprinkle with caraway seeds and salt. Cover and cook over medium heat for about 20 minutes. Simmer for another 10 minutes. Before serving, sprinkle with finely chopped parsley.

Grandma's Tip: To refine, cook 1 teaspoon dill seeds and 2 bay leaves with the cabbage. To thicken broth, blend 1 teaspoon flour with 2 tablespoons water and stir into the hot cabbage. Serve with boiled or parsley potatoes, German hamburgers, sausages, bratwurst, or pork chops.

Yield: 4 servings

Spinach (Spinatgemüse)

2 tablespoons margarine or butter
2 medium onions
2 pounds spinach
1 cup water
1 tablespoon flour
1 teaspoon salt
1 teaspoon pepper
2 tablespoons liquid whipping cream

Wash and clean spinach leaves. In a pot, bring water to a boil. Add the spinach, sprinkle with salt, and boil for about 2 minutes. Strain spinach and save spinach broth. With a grinder or electric blender, finely mince spinach with 1 onion.

In a skillet, melt margarine. Brown finely chopped onion and sprinkle with flour. Stir and slowly blend spinach broth into the mixture. Bring to a boil. Add the finely minced spinach and fold in liquid whipping cream. Sprinkle with salt and pepper. Cook for another 5 minutes over medium heat.

Grandma's Tip: To refine spinach, add 2 tablespoons finely minced parsley. If desired, mince only one-third of the spinach in the electric blender. Finely chop the rest of the spinach and combine later with blended spinach. Serve with fried or scrambled eggs, boiled or buttered parsley potatoes.

Yield: 4 servings

Sauerkraut (Sauerkraut)

1½	pounds packed, refrigerated sauerkraut
1	finely chopped onion
½	tablespoons caraway seeds
½	peeled, chopped apple (without seeds)
½	tablespoon dill seeds
1	potato
1	cup beef broth
2	bay leaves

Rinse sauerkraut with cold water through a strainer. In a pot, bring broth to a boil. Add sauerkraut and combine with bay leaves, onion, caraway seeds, apple, and dill seeds. Reduce heat and cook over medium heat for about 15 minutes. Meanwhile, peel potato and shred into the sauerkraut. Cover and cook over medium heat for another 30 minutes. Reduce heat and simmer over low heat 1 hour.

Grandma's Tip: Sauerkraut tastes especially good when you reheat it. To make it more flavorful, stir in 2 tablespoons of packaged brown gravy mix. Serve with mashed potatoes and bratwurst.

Yield: 4–5 servings

Red Cabbage (Rotkraut)

1   medium head fresh red cabbage
3   whole cloves or ½ tablespoon grated cloves
1   cup beef broth
2   bay leaves
1   medium peeled and cut apple
1   tablespoon raisins
1   medium chopped onion
2   tablespoons brown gravy mix
dash   salt
½   tablespoon sugar

Cut cabbage into fine strips and rinse under cold water in a strainer. In a pot, bring broth to a boil. Add the cabbage and combine with onion, salt, sugar, raisins, apple, bay leaves, and cloves. Reduce heat, cover, and cook over medium heat for about 20 minutes. Bring to a boil again and blend in the brown gravy mix. Simmer over low heat for another hour or longer.

Grandma's Tip: Cabbage usually tastes better when it is reheated. For variety, add about 3 tablespoons finely cut fresh or canned pineapple. Serve with mashed or boiled potatoes, dumplings, rouladen, schnitzel, pork chops, German hamburgers, or bratwurst.

Yield: 4 servings

Chapter 10
Meat Dishes

Chapter 10

Meat Dishes

Fleischgerichte

Game (Wildbret)

It is important to remove skin of game before processing the meat. Game should be marinaded for at least 1–2 days before cooking. To lard meat, poke holes into the meat with a knife and stuff holes with bacon pieces.

Jaeger Sauce (Jägersoße)

1	cup fresh (or canned) mushrooms, chopped
1½	cups water
½	onion, diced
1	package brown gravy mix
2	tablespoons margarine
2	tablespoons finely chopped parsley

In a large saucepan, melt margarine. Add onion and mushrooms and fry until golden. Add water, bring to a boil, and blend in the brown gravy mix. Reduce heat and cook over medium heat for about 5–10 minutes. Before serving, sprinkle with finely chopped parsley.

Grandma's Tip: Pour this sauce over schnitzel and serve with potatoes and a fresh garden salad.

Yield: 3–4 servings

Marinade for Game 1

- 1   cup oil
- ½   tablespoon pepper
- ½   tablespoon salt
- ½   tablespoon grated juniper berries

Combine all ingredients and rub into the meat on all sides. Cover meat and set aside in the refrigerator for about 1 day.

Marinade for Game 2

- 1   cup water
- 1   cup vinegar
- 3–4   peppercorns
- 2   bay leaves
- 4–5   juniper berries
- 1   branch thyme (optional)
- 1   branch basil (optional)

In a pot, bring all ingredients to a boil. Remove from stove, cool, and set meat into the marinade for 1–2 days in the refrigerator.

Marinade for Game 3

Marinade meat in about 2 cups buttermilk for 1–2 days.

Marinade for Game 4

Heat about 2 cups red wine with 2 bay leaves, 2–3 peppercorns, and 3–4 juniper berries. Cool and place meat in this marinade for 2–3 days.

Wild Boar in Red Wine Sauce
(Wildschwein in Rotweinsoße)

2–3	pounds boar-hog meat without bones
1½	cups beef broth
1½	cups red wine
1	onion, sliced
2	cloves garlic
2–3	sticks carrots
2–3	sticks celery
6–8	peppercorns
dash	salt
2	bay leaves
2	slices dried pumpernickel (dark bread)
1½	tablespoon cinnamon sugar
1	stick cinnamon
2	tablespoons butter or margarine
3	cloves or 1 teaspoon clove powder
3–4	juniper berries
¼	pound bacon

After processing meat, rinse under cold water and pat dry with a paper towel. Lard meat with diced bacon cubes (about every 2–3 inches). In a roasting pan, blend broth with wine. Add diced celery, diced carrots, sliced onion, bay leaves, peppercorns, cloves or clove powder, juniper berries, garlic, and cinnamon stick. Sprinkle meat on both sides with salt and place in the wine marinade. Cover and simmer over low heat for about 3 hours or until meat seems almost tender. Turn meat every now and then, so marinade can soak into both sides. Remove meat from roasting pan, pat dry, and cut into ½ to 1-inch-thick slices (or roast can be left whole). Strain gravy through a strainer. Put sliced meat in a casserole dish and drizzle with 1½ cup strained broth. Sprinkle with grated bread and cinnamon sugar. Drizzle with melted butter or margarine. Bake in a 320 degree preheated oven for another 40–50 minutes, basting occasionally.

Grandma's Tip: Sprinkle with fresh, finely chopped parsley and serve with dumplings, buttered potatoes, parsley potatoes, vegetables, red cabbage, or fresh garden salad.

Yield: 4–5 servings

Venison in Sour Cream Current Sauce
(Wild in Saure-Sahne Preiselbeersoße)

about	3–4 pounds deer meat
¼	pound bacon
1	cup sour cream
1	cup dry white wine
dash	pepper
dash	salt
3–4	peppercorns
1	bay leaf
1	tablespoon cornstarch or flour
1/3	cup currant jelly or cranberry sauce
¼	cup melted margarine
½	cup beef broth
2	garlic cloves

Rinse prepared meat under cold water. Cut into 2-inch-thick slices. Tenderize and sprinkle with salt and pepper on both sides. In a roasting pan, melt margarine. Lard meat with bacon pieces and brown on both sides until golden. Blend together sour cream, ¼ cup broth, and 1 cup white wine. Pour mixture over meat in a roasting pan. Bake uncovered in a 350 degree oven for about 30 minutes. Add garlic, peppercorns, and bay leaf. Baste occasionally so meat will not dry out. Blend ¼ cup broth with flour and stir into the heated sauce. Bake for another 30–40 minutes. Turn meat every once in a while and blend in jelly or cranberry sauce. Remove meat from sauce. Blend sauce again with a wire whisk and pour over meat.

Grandma's Tip: As a variation, try red wine. For variety, brown chopped celery root and 1 stick chopped carrot with the meat. Try blending 1 tablespoon lemon juice or vinegar into the sauce. Serve dish with dumplings, red cabbage, fresh tossed salad, or any kind of buttered vegetable. If desired, sprinkle with about 2 tablespoons fresh chopped parsley.

Yield: 4–5 servings

Goulash (Gulasch)

1½–2	pounds beef or pork stew meat, finely chopped
1	green bell pepper
1½	onions
¼	cup flour
1	tablespoon caraway seeds
4	tomatoes, diced
1	potato
dash	pepper
dash	salt
dash	paprika
2	tablespoons finely chopped parsley
4	tablespoons margarine
2	cups water
½	package brown gravy mix
2	carrots

In a pot, melt the margarine. Add the meat and brown until light golden brown. Sprinkle with salt, pepper, paprika, and flour. Clean and cut bell peppers into thin slices. Add bell peppers, chopped onion, tomatoes, and chopped carrots to the meat. Cook over medium heat for about 3–5 minutes. Add the water. Peel and cut potatoes into cubes and add to the meat mixture. Sprinkle with caraway seeds. Cover and cook over medium heat for about 1½ hours. Bring everything to a boil again and blend in the brown gravy mix. Simmer for another half hour. Before serving, sprinkle with parsley.

Grandma's Tip: Add a little water to make more sauce. The longer goulash simmers, the more tender the meat becomes. Stir occasionally. For a more flavorful sauce, add 2–3 bay leaves and cook with the sauce.

Stuffed Beef Rolls (Rouladen)

6	thin slices of beef round
2	tablespoons mustard
dash	salt and pepper
dash	paprika
12	slices of pickles
6	slices bacon
½	onion, sliced
½	onion, chopped
2	carrots, chopped
2	fresh tomatoes, diced
2	cups water
3–4	tablespoons margarine
1	package brown gravy mix

Tenderize each slice of beef round. Sprinkle both sides with pepper, salt, and paprika. Spread only one side with mustard. Lay flat on a countertop, with mustard side facing up. Layer each slice with 2 pickles, 2–3 slices of the onion, and 1 chopped piece of bacon. Roll up with the filling and tighten with a thread or toothpick. In a roasting pan or large skillet, melt margarine. Add rouladen and brown on both sides until golden. Add tomatoes, chopped onion, and sliced carrots and cook over medium heat for about 5 minutes. Add 1 cup water and continue cooking over medium heat for another 15 minutes. Meanwhile, with a fork, pierce holes into the meat and occasionally turn rouladen over. Now fill with rest of the water and simmer for another 2 hours or until meat is tender. Bring to a boil again. Blend in the brown gravy mix, reduce heat and cook over medium heat for another 10 minutes. If the sauce reduces too much, add a little water so the desired amount of sauce is still available.

Grandma's Tip: Instead of using onions, pickles, and bacon, stuff rouladen with hamburger meat spiced with a dash of pepper, salt, paprika, caraway seeds, and chopped onions. To thicken sauce, blend 1 tablespoon cornstarch or flour with 2 tablespoons water. Bring sauce to a boil and stir. Serve with red cabbage and dumplings, if desired. Also you can blend 1 tablespoon finely chopped parsley into the sauce.

Yield: 4–5 serving

Stuffed Cabbage (Krautrouladen)

1	pound hamburger meat
1	medium head of white cabbage (about 10 medium leaves)
dash	salt
dash	paprika
dash	pepper
1	onion
2	carrots, chopped
2	fresh tomatoes
3	cups saltwater
2	cups beef broth
3	tablespoons liquid whipping cream
3	tablespoons margarine
1	tablespoon cornstarch
3	tablespoons cold water
1	egg
4	tablespoons plain bread crumbs
½	tablespoon caraway seeds

In a bowl, mix hamburger meat with salt, paprika, pepper, caraway seeds, bread crumbs, egg, ½ chopped onion, and ¼ head finely shredded cabbage. Mix everything together. Carefully separate whole leaves from the cabbage. In a pot, bring water with salt to a boil. Add leaves of the cabbage and cook over medium heat for about 3–5 minutes or until leaves are tender. Remove from the water, pat leaves dry with a paper towel, and lay out flat on a countertop. Stack 1–2 leaves together and fill each with 3–4 tablespoons of the prepared hamburger meat. Roll up with the filling and wrap with a thread or keep together with a toothpick. In a roasting pan or large skillet, melt the margarine, add cabbage rolls, and brown on both sides until golden. Add carrots, ½ chopped or sliced onion, and diced tomatoes. Cook over medium heat and slowly fill with beef broth. Cover and continue cooking over medium heat for 20 minutes. Reduce heat and simmer for ½ hour. Stir in the liquid whipping cream. To thicken sauce, blend 1 tablespoon cornstarch or flour with 3 tablespoons water and stir into the sauce. Garnish with about 2 tablespoons finely chopped parsley.

Grandma's Tip: After cooking for a while, the liquid will diminish. Add more water until the desired amount of sauce is achieved. Before serving, remove the thread or toothpick. For a more flavorful sauce, add 2–3 bay leaves, ½ package of brown gravy and cook with sauce. Serve with boiled potatoes.

Yield: 4 servings

———————————————

Schnitzel or Pork Chops
(Schnitzel oder Kotletts)

4	boneless pork chops or sliced pork tenderloin
½	cup flour
½	cup plain bread crumbs
dash	salt
dash	pepper
dash	paprika
2	eggs
½	cup oil

Rinse meat under cold water. Pat dry with a paper towel and tenderize on both sides. Sprinkle meat on both sides with salt, pepper, and paprika. Beat the eggs and dip both sides of the meat into the mixture. Roll both sides in flour, then dip into the blended egg again. Now dip both sides into the bread crumbs. In a large skillet, heat the oil and fry the chops on both sides over medium heat for about 20 minutes or until both sides are crisp and golden.

Grandma's Tip: Don't cover the pan while cooking or the meat won't be crispy. After meat is done, pat with a paper towel to remove some of the oil. Serve with potato salad, buttered parsley potatoes, mashed potatoes with gravy, or with a vegetable with hollandaise sauce.

Yield: 3–4 servings

———————————————

Stuffed Peppers (Gefüllte Paprikaschoten)

5	whole green bell peppers
1	finely chopped green bell pepper
½	tablespoon salt
½	tablespoon pepper
½	tablespoon paprika
½	onion, sliced
½	onion, chopped
dash	caraway seeds
2	carrots
3	tomatoes
1½	pounds hamburger meat
2	tablespoons finely chopped parsley
1	package brown gravy mix
3	cups water
4	tablespoons margarine
4	tablespoons bread crumbs
1	egg

Wash bell peppers. Cut a 1-inch slice from the top of the pepper. Clean out the seeds. Chop 1 pepper into very fine cubes. In a bowl, mix the hamburger meat with salt, pepper, paprika, caraway seeds, ½ finely chopped onion, egg, bread crumbs, and the finely chopped bell pepper. Fill the bell pepper cups with seasoned hamburger. In a roasting pan or large skillet, melt margarine. Add peppers and lightly brown both sides. Add diced tomato, chopped carrots, and sliced onion. If there is any hamburger meat left, add it with the leftover pepper slices. Carefully blend in the water and cook over medium heat for about 20 minutes. Bring to a boil, blend in the brown gravy mix, cover and simmer for another 45 minutes. If desired, continue baking bell peppers for another 20 minutes in a 320 degree preheated oven. Sprinkle with finely chopped parsley.

Grandma's Tip: For a richer sauce, add 2 tablespoons liquid whipping cream to the sauce. After cooking, top each pepper with pepper slices. Add more water, if liquid is reducing too fast. For a more flavorful sauce, add 2–3 bay leaves and cook with sauce. Serve with boiled or mashed potatoes.

Yield: 4 servings

German Hamburger (Frikadelle)

1½   pounds hamburger meat
½   cup plus 3 tablespoons bread crumbs
2   eggs
½   tablespoon salt
½   tablespoon pepper
½   tablespoon paprika
1   tablespoon finely chopped parsley
1   teaspoon caraway seeds
½   onion, finely chopped
¼   cup oil

In a bowl, mix hamburger meat with salt, pepper, paprika, 1 egg, 3 tablespoons bread crumbs, finely chopped onion, parsley, and caraway seeds. Form patties with about 4 spoonfuls of meat mixture. Beat the egg. Roll hamburgers in the egg and coat both sides with the bread crumbs. In a large skillet, heat the oil. Add hamburger patties and fry over medium heat on both sides for about 30 minutes or until cooked and golden brown.

Grandma's Tip: If you like your hamburgers more firm, add 1–2 tablespoons of bread crumbs. The hamburgers will be more crispy if you don't cover them. Before serving, pat dry with a paper towel so they won't be too oily. Serve with potato salad, boiled potatoes, bread, a garden salad, or vegetables with hollandaise sauce.

Yield: 4–5 servings

Ribs in Brown Gravy (Rippchen in Soße)

4	pounds beef or pork spare ribs
5	tablespoons mustard
dash	salt
dash	pepper
dash	paprika
1	onion
3	tomatoes
2	carrots
2–3	bay leaves
3	cups water
1	package brown gravy
5	tablespoons margarine or oil

Rinse ribs under cold water. Pat dry with a paper towel and cut into 3–4 inch thick slices. Spread ribs with mustard. Sprinkle with salt, pepper, and paprika. In a roasting pan, melt margarine and brown ribs on both sides until golden. Add diced tomatoes, carrots, and onion. Cook over medium heat for about 5 minutes. Slowly add water and bay leaves. Bring to a boil again and blend in the brown gravy mix. Cover and cook over medium heat for about 1 hour. Add more water if the sauce becomes too thick. Place in a preheated 320 degree oven for another 1 hour, uncovered. Stir occasionally. Before serving, sprinkle with finely chopped parsley.

Grandma's Tip: For very tender meat, continue cooking ribs up to 4 hours, basting occasionally. If desired, add 2 cloves finely minced garlic. Serve with potato dumplings, mashed potatoes, or boiled potatoes and a fresh garden salad.

Tip for barbecued ribs: In a pot with 8 cups water, 1 tablespoon salt, dash pepper, 1 sliced onion, and 3 bay leaves, cook ribs over medium heat for about 1 hour. Remove from water and blend with a favorite barbeque sauce.

Yield: 4–6 servings

Tender Roast (Schweine-oder Rinderbraten)

2   pounds beef or pork roast
4   tablespoons mustard
3   bay leaves
2   tomatoes, diced
2   carrots, chopped
1   onion, chopped
dash   salt
dash   pepper
dash   paprika
3   cups water
1   package brown gravy mix
4   tablespoons margarine
3   tablespoons liquid whipping cream

Rinse meat under cold water. Pat dry with a paper towel. Spread all sides with mustard. Sprinkle with salt, pepper, and paprika. In a roasting pan, melt margarine and brown roast on both sides until golden. Add diced tomatoes, onion, and carrots. Cook over medium heat for about 5 minutes. Slowly add water and bring to a boil. Blend in brown gravy mix. Add bay leaves, cover, and cook over medium heat for about 1 hour. If sauce is too thick, add some more water. Cover and bake in a preheated 320 degree oven for 1 hour, basting occasionally. Remove cover and brown roast on both sides for about 20 minutes. Blend in the liquid whipping cream and stir. If desired, sprinkle with 2 tablespoons finely chopped parsley.

Grandma's Tip: For very tender roast, continue cooking up to 4 hours. While cooking the roast, poke several holes on both sides of the roast with a fork. Serve with dumplings, potatoes, and vegetables.

Yield: 4–5 servings

Fried Liver (Gebratene Leber)

       2   pounds beef or pork liver
      ¼   cup flour
    dash   salt
    dash   pepper
    1–2   slices onions
       1   apple, peeled and diced
       5   tablespoons oil

Rinse liver under cold water and pat dry with a paper towel. Sprinkle with flour, salt, and pepper. In a large skillet, heat the oil. Add liver and brown on both sides until golden. Add the diced apple and onions, continue frying over medium heat for another 20 to 30 minutes. Once in a while, turn the liver.

Grandma's Tip: If desired, cut liver into small pieces before cooking. Serve over mashed potatoes or with rice.

Yield: 4 servings

Meatloaf (Hackbraten)

       2   pounds hamburger
       2   eggs
      ½   tablespoon salt
      ½   tablespoon pepper
      ½   tablespoon paprika
      ½   cup and 4 tablespoons plain bread crumbs
      ½   tablespoons caraway seeds
       1   tablespoon finely chopped parsley
       3   cups water
       1   package brown gravy mix
       1   diced tomato
       2   carrots, chopped
       1   onion, finely chopped
       5   tablespoons margarine
       2   tablespoons mustard

In a bowl, mix hamburger meat with 1 egg, salt, pepper, mustard, paprika, 4 tablespoons bread crumbs, ½ chopped onion, parsley, and caraway seeds. Form into an oval shape and dip both sides into 1 blended egg and ½ cup bread crumbs. In a roasting pan, melt margarine and brown meatloaf on both sides until golden. Add ½ sliced onion, carrots, and tomatoes. Cook over medium heat for about 5 minutes. Slowly add water, bring to a boil, and carefully blend in the brown gravy mix. Cover and cook over medium heat for about 30 minutes. Remove cover and bake in a preheated 320 degree oven for about 1 hour. Turn meatloaf once in a while until crisp and golden on both sides. Baste with a ladle full of gravy every now and then.

Grandma's Tip: The longer you cook the meatloaf, the tastier it will be. Add water if sauce becomes too thick. About 10 minutes before serving, blend in 3 tablespoons liquid whipping cream, if desired. Sprinkle sauce with fresh, finely chopped parsley, if desired. Serve with dumplings, boiled parsley potatoes, mashed potatoes, or a vegetable.

Yield: 4–5 servings

Filled Meatloaf (Gefüllter Hackbraten)

Prepare meatloaf like before, but fold 2 boiled eggs into the center of the meatloaf.

Goulash Casserole (Gulasch Auflauf)

1½	pounds beef or pork stew
¼	pound bacon (diced)
4	tablespoons margarine
1	onion, sliced
2	bay leaves
3	cups beef broth
¼	pound mushrooms
½	green bell pepper
½	red bell pepper
2	tomatoes, diced
1	tablespoon caraway seeds
dash	salt
dash	pepper
dash	paprika
2	potatoes, diced
2	tablespoons flour

Rinse meat under cold water and pat dry with a paper towel. In a roasting pan, melt margarine. Add meat and bacon. Sprinkle with flour, salt, pepper, and paprika. Brown until golden. Add potatoes, mushrooms, onion, sliced bell peppers, and tomatoes. Cook over medium heat for about 5 minutes. Slowly add the broth. Add bay leaves and sprinkle with caraway seeds. Cover and cook over medium heat for about 1 hour. Stir occasionally. Bake uncovered in a 320 degree preheated oven for another 30 minutes. Sprinkle with finely chopped parsley.

Grandma's Tip: For a creamier taste, blend in 3 tablespoons liquid whipping cream. To thicken sauce, blend 1 tablespoon flour with 3 tablespoons water and blend into sauce or, instead of using flour, use ½ package brown gravy mix. To make goulash more flavorful, fold 2 cloves finely minced garlic into the meat.

Yield: 4 servings

Hamburger Casserole (Hackfleisch Auflauf)

1	pound hamburger
1	red or green bell pepper
2	cloves garlic, finely minced
½	pound mushrooms
½	tablespoon caraway seeds
1½	cups water
1	onion, finely chopped
dash	salt
dash	pepper
dash	paprika
1	package brown gravy mix
1	cup shredded mozzarella cheese

In a large skillet, brown the hamburger and strain the grease. Cut washed mushrooms and bell pepper into slices and brown with the hamburger over medium heat for about 5 minutes. Sprinkle with salt, pepper, caraway seeds and paprika. Fold in the diced onion and the finely minced garlic cloves. Add water, bring to a boil, and blend in brown gravy mix. Put into a casserole dish, sprinkle with shredded cheese, and bake in a 350 degree oven for about 15 minutes.

Grandma's Tip: If desired, combine the meat with several other vegetables, like chopped carrots, diced tomatoes, chopped celery, or green onions. Serve with rice, noodles, or boiled potatoes.

Yield: 4 servings

Creamed Cutlets (Sahne Geschnetzeltes)

        1½ pound tenderloin or veal cutlets
        ¼   pound bacon
        1   onion
        ½   pound fresh mushrooms
        ¼   cup dry white wine
    dash   pepper
    dash   salt
        1½ cups water
        1   cup beaten whipping cream
        2   tablespoons finely chopped parsley
        1   package brown gravy mix
        2   cloves garlic, finely minced

In a large skillet, lightly fry bacon. Add sliced pork tenderloin or veal cutlets and brown over medium heat until golden. Add mushrooms, sliced onion, and garlic cloves. Sprinkle with salt and pepper. Cover and cook over medium heat for about 5 minutes. Sprinkle with brown gravy mix. Slowly add wine and water and stir rapidly. Cover and cook over low heat for another 30 minutes. Before serving, fold in whipping cream and sprinkle with parsley.

Grandma's Tip: Instead of using ¼ cup wine, use ½ cup wine and only 1 cup water. Serve with potatoes or dumplings.

Yield: 4 servings

Sour Pickled Roast (Sauerbraten)

        3   pounds beef roast
        3   tablespoons mustard
    dash   salt
    dash   pepper
    dash   paprika
        1   onion
        1   tomato, diced
        4   tablespoons margarine
        1½ cups water
        3   tablespoons liquid whipping cream
        ½   package brown gravy mix

Marinade:

        2   cups red wine
        1   cup vinegar
        1   teaspoon powdered cloves or 2 whole cloves
        2   teaspoons pepper or 4 peppercorns
        2   carrots, sliced
        1   tablespoon mustard
        1   teaspoon salt
        2   teaspoons sugar
        1   sliced onion
        2   bay leaves

In a large bowl, combine all ingredients for the marinade. Add the roast. Cover and put into refrigerator for 2 to 3 days. Once in a while, turn roast over so marinade soaks into both sides of roast. Remove roast from marinade and pat dry with a paper towel. Spread with mustard; sprinkle with salt, pepper, and paprika. In a roasting pan, melt margarine. Add roast and brown on both sides until golden. Pour half the marinade over the roast. Add diced tomato, diced onion, stir, cover, and put into a 350 degree preheated oven. Bake roast for about 30 minutes and fold in the rest of the marinade. Cover and bake again for another hour. Turn roast over occasionally. Remove roast from marinade, set aside, and blend water into the marinade. On the stove, bring everything to a boil. Add brown gravy mix and stir. Place roast back into the gravy and bake in the 350 degree oven again for another 10–15 minutes. Before serving, fold in liquid whipping cream.

Grandma's Tip: Instead of using 2 cups red wine and 1 cup vinegar, use 2 cups vinegar and 1 cup water. To refine, add ½ cup fresh or canned mushrooms and ½ chopped celery root for the marinade. Sprinkle with finely fresh chopped parsley and serve with dumplings or potatoes and fresh cucumber or garden salad.

Yield: 4–5 servings

Bratwurst in Beer Batter (Bratwurst in Bierteig)

4–6	bratwurst
4	tablespoons melted margarine
½	tablespoon sugar
dash	salt
dash	pepper
½	tablespoon lemon juice
1	cup beer
½	cup oil
1	cup flour

Rinse bratwurst under cold water and pat dry with a paper towel. In a skillet, heat the oil and fry bratwurst until light golden on all sides. In a bowl, mix flour, melted margarine, beer, salt, sugar, pepper, and lemon juice and set aside for about 20 minutes. Remove bratwurst from skillet. Pat dry and dip all sides into the beer batter. Heat the oil again and fry bratwurst over medium heat for another 10–15 minutes or until batter turns golden brown.

Grandma's Tip: If batter does not stick to bratwurst, coat them twice. Oil needs to be hot before adding the bratwurst. Serve with potato salad, mashed potatoes, or fresh garden salad with oil or sour cream dressing.

Yield: 4–5 servings

Other Tips for cooking your bratwurst: For a better taste, soak bratwurst in cold water before cooking for about 5 minutes. To give barbecued bratwurst a better taste, drizzle bratwurst with some beer while on the grill. For a spicier taste, spread bratwurst with oil and mustard while cooking on the grill.

Paprika Cutlets (Paprika Geschnetzeltes)

1–2	pounds veal or pork tenderloin
1	green pepper, sliced
1	red bell pepper, sliced
1	onion, sliced
2	cups beef broth
dash	salt
3	tablespoons tomato paste
1	tomato, diced
dash	pepper
dash	paprika
3	tablespoons liquid whipping cream
½	package brown gravy mix
2	tablespoons margarine
2	tablespoons finely chopped parsley

In a large skillet or roasting pan, melt margarine. Slice the meat and brown on both sides until golden. Add sliced onion, bell peppers, and diced tomato. Sprinkle with pepper, salt, and paprika. Cook everything over medium heat for about 5 minutes. Add broth. Blend in tomato paste. Bring everything to a boil and fold in the brown gravy mix. Cover and cook over medium heat for about 30 minutes. Stir occasionally. Add whipping cream and continue cooking for another 5 minutes. Before serving, sprinkle with finely chopped parsley.

Grandma's Tip: For variety, fry about ½ cup sliced fresh mushrooms with bell pepper. Serve with rice or potatoes.

Yield: 4 servings

Smoked Pork Chops with Sauerkraut
(Geräucherte Kotletts in Sauerkraut)

4–5	smoked pork chops or tenderloin
1½	pounds refrigerated sauerkraut
½	onion, sliced
2	bay leaves
1	teaspoon sugar
dash	salt
dash	pepper
½	tablespoon dill seeds
½	package brown gravy mix
3–5	juniper berries
½	apple, diced
1	potato
2	tablespoons margarine
1½	cups water

Rinse sauerkraut through a strainer under cold water. In a pot, bring 1 cup water to a boil. Add the strained sauerkraut and combine with dill seeds, sugar, bay leaves, sliced onion, salt, pepper, juniper berries, shredded potato, and diced apple. Stir together and cook everything over medium heat for about 30–45 minutes. Meanwhile, blend ½ cup water with brown gravy mix and fold into the cooking sauerkraut. In a skillet, melt margarine. Add chops or tenderloins and brown on both sides until golden. Pour sauerkraut into a casserole or baking dish. Top with chops or tenderloins and put into a preheated 350 degree oven. Bake for another 20 minutes.

Grandma's Tip: Serve with mashed potatoes and gravy.

Yield: 4–5 servings

Stuffed Cauliflower (Gefüllter Blumenkohl)

1	large head of cauliflower
1	pound hamburger
½	onion
dash	salt
dash	pepper
dash	paprika
1	teaspoon caraway seeds
½	tablespoon nutmeg
3	slices cheese
1	egg
1/3	cup bread crumbs
1¼	cup bechamel sauce
2	tablespoons butter

Rinse cauliflower under cold water. Remove leaves and make a large well at the stem and leaf side. In a mixing bowl, mix hamburger with salt, pepper, paprika, egg, chopped onion, caraway seeds, and bread crumbs. Fill in the well of the cauliflower with the meat mixture. Spread cauliflower with butter and sprinkle with nutmeg. Set into a baking dish or roasting pan. Pour bechamel sauce over the top and bake in a preheated 350 degree oven. Cover and bake for about 20 minutes. Remove cover, reduce heat to 320 degrees, layer with cheese, and bake again for another 20–30 minutes. Baste often with the sauce. Cover the top of cauliflower with a piece of aluminum foil so it will not burn.

Grandma's Tip: If sauce becomes too thick, blend in about ¼ cup water or broth. Sprinkle with fresh, finely chopped parsley and serve with boiled, parsley, or mashed potatoes.

Yield: 4–5 servings

Chapter 11
Chicken and Fish Dishes

Chapter 11

Chicken and Fish Dishes

Huhn-und Fischgerichte

Chicken Fillets (Hühnerfillets)

4–5	chicken breast fillets
dash	salt
dash	paprika
dash	pepper
1½	tablespoons lemon juice
1/3	cup oil
1	egg
½	cup bread crumbs or flour

Rinse fillets under cold water and pat dry with a paper towel. Sprinkle with salt, pepper, and paprika. Drizzle both sides with lemon juice. Beat the egg and dip fillets. Toss both sides in the flour or bread crumbs. In a skillet, heat the oil and add fillets. Brown both sides until golden. Reduce heat and cook both sides, uncovered, over medium heat for about 30 minutes. Keep turning the chicken.

Grandma's Tip: Serve fillets with potato salad or other salad. Instead of using chicken breast fillets, you can use any other parts of the chicken prepared in the same way.

Yield: 4 servings

Stuffed Chicken (Gefülltes Huhn)

1	whole chicken
dash	salt
dash	pepper
1–2	tablespoons lemon juice
3	tablespoons margarine

For the stuffing:

1	pound hamburger
dash	salt
dash	pepper
1	egg
½	onion
1	slice white bread
1	tablespoon finely chopped parsley

For the sauce:

2½	cups water
1	package chicken gravy mix
1	stalk celery, chopped
1	carrot, chopped
1	tablespoon finely chopped parsley
1	onion, sliced

Rinse chicken under cold water and pat dry with a paper towel. Sprinkle with salt and pepper. Drizzle with lemon juice. In a bowl, mix the hamburger with salt, pepper, chopped onion, egg, parsley, and crumbled bread slice. Place stuffing into the chicken and tighten with a thread. In a roasting pan, melt margarine. Add chicken and brown on both sides until golden. Blend water with chicken gravy mix and slowly pour over the chicken. Add celery, carrot, and the sliced onion. Cover, place in a preheated 350 degree oven and bake for about 30 minutes. Turn chicken over and bake again for another 30 minutes. Remove the cover, turn over the chicken, and bake again for 40 minutes. Cover the top of chicken with a piece of aluminum foil so it won't burn. Stir gravy occasionally. Before serving, sprinkle with fresh, finely chopped parsley.

Grandma's Tip: To refine, add 3–4 finely chopped mushrooms. Serve with rice, mashed potatoes, or dumplings. Chicken also can be seasoned with a dash of paprika.

Note: Always rinse chicken thoroughly under cold water before cooking. To tenderize fried or BBQ chicken, boil chicken first in a pot with about 2 cups water, dash salt, dash pepper, and a few bay leaves over medium heat for about 20 minutes.

Yield: 4 servings

———————————————

Fried Chicken Halves *(Gebratenes Huhn)*

2	chicken halves
2	eggs
1	cup plain bread crumbs
dash	salt
dash	pepper
dash	paprika
1	lemon
1	cup oil

Rinse chicken under cold water and pat dry with a paper towel. Sprinkle both sides with pepper, salt, and paprika. Drizzle with lemon juice. Dip into blended egg and roll in bread crumbs. In a large skillet, heat the oil and fry chicken over medium heat on both sides for about 30 minutes or until cooked.

Grandma's Tip: Do not cover skillet or the chicken won't be crisp. Serve chicken with potato salad and lettuce.

Yield: 2–4 servings

———————————————

Chicken Fricassee (Hühnerfricassee)

1	whole chicken
1½	tablespoons salt
6	cups water
2	carrots, chopped
2	stalks celery, chopped
15	ounces canned asparagus, strained
1	tablespoon lemon juice
dash	sugar
1	egg yolk
3	tablespoons margarine or butter
3–4	peppercorns
1	tablespoon flour
dash	pepper
1	onion
2	bay leaves

Rinse chicken under cold water and pat dry with a paper towel. In a large pot, bring water to a boil. Add chicken, 1 tablespoon salt, sliced onion, peppercorns, and bay leaves. Cover and cook over medium heat for about 1 hour. Add celery and carrots and cook for another half hour. In a pot, melt margarine. Sprinkle with flour and slowly blend in 2 cups of chicken broth (removed from the cooking chicken). With a wire whisk blend in the egg yolk. Drizzle with lemon juice. Sprinkle with salt, pepper, and sugar and stir. Add finely chopped asparagus and stir again. Now strain broth from chicken and cut chicken into pieces. Add celery, carrots, and chicken pieces to broth and simmer at low heat for another 5 minutes.

Grandma's Tip: To refine, add ¼ cup strained, canned mushrooms, 3–4 capers and, if desired, 3 tablespoons dry white wine. Sprinkle fricassee with paprika and serve with rice or potatoes.

Yield: 4 servings

Chicken Fillet Stew (Hühnerfillet Stew)

3–4	chicken breasts, washed and cleaned
½	green bell pepper, sliced
½	red bell pepper, sliced
½	onion
2	green onions
dash	pepper
dash	salt
dash	paprika
1	tablespoon lemon juice
1	tablespoon flour
1½	cups chicken broth
2	tablespoons margarine

Rinse chicken under cold water. Pat dry with a paper towel and cut into slices. In a large skillet, melt margarine. Add chicken and bell peppers. Sprinkle with salt, pepper, and paprika. Drizzle with lemon juice. Add finely sliced onion. Stir everything together and brown over medium heat for about 15 minutes. Sprinkle with flour. Slowly blend in the chicken broth, cover, and cook over medium heat for another 20 minutes. Add finely cut green onion and simmer for 10 minutes.

Grandma's Tip: If you want to serve this dish with more gravy, just add ½ water and ½ package of chicken gravy. Serve with either rice or mashed potatoes.

Yield: 4 servings

Paprika Chicken (Paprika Huhn)

1	whole chicken, cut into pieces
dash	salt
dash	pepper
dash	paprika
1	tablespoon lemon juice
1	bell pepper
1	onion, finely chopped
1	clove garlic, finely minced
½	pound bacon
1	cup chicken broth
1	tablespoon flour
2	tablespoons tomato paste
3	tablespoons margarine

Rinse chicken under cold water and pat dry with a paper towel. Sprinkle all sides with pepper, salt, and paprika. Drizzle with lemon juice. In a roasting pan, melt 3 tablespoons margarine. Add chicken pieces and brown all sides until golden. In a separate skillet, brown finely diced bacon until golden. Add cleaned and sliced bell pepper, onion, and garlic and cook over medium heat for about 5 minutes. Sprinkle with flour and slowly stir in chicken broth and tomato paste. Carefully fold everything together and cook over medium heat for another 5 minutes. Pour this sauce over the chicken, cover roasting pan, and bake in a 350 degree preheated oven for about 45 minutes.

Grandma's Tip: If you want to serve this dish with more gravy, add ½ cup water and ½ package chicken gravy mix. Instead of using tomato paste, try adding 2–3 diced tomatoes and another red bell pepper. Serve this dish with rice, boiled potatoes, or mashed potatoes. Sprinkle with 2 tablespoons finely chopped parsley.

Yield: 4 servings

Beer Marinaded Chicken (Huhn in Biermarinade)

1	whole chicken, cut into pieces
dash	salt
dash	pepper
¼	pound bacon
3	green onions
1	tablespoon thyme
1	tablespoon marjoram
1	tablespoon dill or parsley
2	cloves garlic
2/3	cup liquid whipping cream
2	tablespoons margarine
3	cups beer
1	onion, sliced
½	lemon
1	tablespoon flour
4–6	peppercorns
2	bay leaves

Rinse chicken under cold water and pat dry with a paper towel. Sprinkle with salt and pepper. Drizzle with lemon juice. In a roasting pan, combine beer with onion, garlic, peppercorns, chopped green onion, thyme, marjoram, and bay leaves. Add chicken parts; cover and refrigerate for about 1 day. Place all ingredients in a separate dish. Remove chicken parts with a spatula. In a roasting pan, melt margarine and finely cut bacon pieces. Add the chicken and brown on all sides until golden. Sprinkle with flour and slowly add the beer marinade. Cover and cook over medium heat for about 30 minutes. Remove from stove, stir in liquid whipping cream, and bake uncovered in a preheated 320 degree oven for another 20 minutes. Turn chicken periodically. Before serving, sprinkle with finely chopped dill or parsley.

Grandma's Tip: If you need more gravy, mix ½ cup water with ¼ package chicken gravy mix and blend into marinade. Serve this dish with a fresh garden salad, rice, or boiled or mashed potatoes. While marinading, turn chicken every now and then.

Yield: 4 serving

Stuffed Thueringer Duck (Gefüllte Thüringer Ente)

1	dressed duck
2	onions
2	cloves garlic, diced
1	teaspoon marjoram
1	teaspoon grated thyme
2	stalks celery
1	carrot
2	tablespoons finely chopped parsley
1	green onion
2	cups beef broth
3	tablespoons margarine
5	potatoes
6	cups water with ½ tablespoon salt
1	slice white toast
1	tablespoon flour
dash	pepper
dash	salt
2	branches fresh thyme
¼	pound bacon

Rinse the duck inside and out under cold water and pat dry with a paper towel. In a pot, bring potatoes to a boil in the salt water. Cook over medium heat until done. Remove from water; peel and cut into cubes. In a skillet, brown chopped bacon with chopped onion, 1 minced garlic clove, chopped green onion, bread cubes and 1 chopped celery stick. Sprinkle with parsley, salt, pepper, thyme, and marjoram. Stuff duck with the filling and sew together with a thread. In a roasting pan, melt margarine. Add duck and brown on all sides until golden. Add chopped carrot, chopped celery, and 1 sliced onion. Sprinkle with salt, pepper, and flour. Slowly blend in 1 cup beef broth and carefully stir. Add the other diced garlic clove, bring to a boil, cover and cook over medium heat for about 20 minutes. Turn duck over, fill with the rest of the broth. Add about 2 branches fresh thyme. Cover and cook again over medium heat for another 20 minutes. Remove roasting pan from stove top and bake uncovered in a 350 degree preheated oven for 40 minutes. Turn duck over and brown duck uncovered for another 40 minutes. Occasionally baste duck with a ladle full of gravy and stir. To avoid burning, cover the very top of the duck with a piece of aluminum foil. Before serving, remove grease.

Grandma's Tip: Baste during the whole cooking process, so the duck will remain juicy. To refine, add ½ cup dry white wine. To expand the amount of gravy, blend in 1 cup water with ½ package chicken gravy mix. Serve with any kind of potato dumplings, mashed potatoes, red cabbage, buttered vegetable, and/or tossed garden salad.

Yield: 4 servings

Chicken in Wine Broth *(Huhn in Weinsoße)*

1	whole chicken, cut into pieces
2	tablespoons margarine
4	green onions
1	tablespoon flour
dash	pepper
dash	salt
2	cloves garlic, finely minced
½	onion, sliced
1	cup dry white wine
1	cup beef broth
1	tablespoon lemon juice
1	tablespoon finely chopped parsley

Rinse chicken pieces under cold water and pat dry with a paper towel. In a roasting pan, melt margarine. Add chicken pieces and fry on all sides until golden. Sprinkle with pepper and salt. Drizzle with lemon juice. Add garlic, finely chopped green onions (with the green part), and finely sliced onion. Cook over medium heat for 5–10 minutes. Stir continually. Sprinkle with flour and slowly add broth and wine. Cover and bake in a 350 degree preheated oven for about 45 minutes. Remove cover and continue baking for another 20 minutes. Stir occasionally. Before serving, sprinkle with parsley.

Grandma's Tip: To refine the taste, blend in 1 teaspoon sugar. Serve with rice or boiled potatoes.

Yield: 3–4 servings

F ish makes a very easily digested and nutritious dish with a lot of vitally important nutrients, such as iodine, calcium, iron, protein, etc. If you prepare fresh fish, remove scales from tail to head. To make the scaling process easier, scald fish with hot water first. Do not remove scales from fish such as trout or carp before cooking. Always cut fish open from head to tail and remove entrails. Wash in cold water and marinate in vinegar or lemon juice. Always poach fish in only a small amount of liquid, using it's own juices as much as possible. Fish is done when you are able to remove the fins.

Poached Fish (Gedämpfter Fisch)

2	pounds fresh or frozen fish (like trout, haddock, or perch)
2	tablespoons butter
1	onion
1	clove minced garlic
1	tablespoon finely chopped parsley
1½	tablespoons lemon juice
dash	salt
dash	pepper
2	cups salt water

Rinse fish under cold water and pat dry with a paper towel. Sprinkle with salt and drizzle with lemon juice. In a large saucepan, bring salt water to a boil. Reduce heat, put fish into a steamer basket, and set basket into the hot saltwater. Sprinkle with chopped or sliced onion, minced garlic, salt, and pepper. Cover and cook over medium heat for about 25–35 minutes. Before serving, drizzle with melted butter, and sprinkle with finely chopped parsley.

Grandma's Tip: Top fish with a fresh herbal sauce, if desired. Serve with potato salad, boiled potatoes, parsley potatoes, any kind buttered vegetable, or fresh tossed salad in an oil or sour cream dressing.

Yield: 4 servings

Breaded Fish Fillets (Panierte Fischfillets)

1½–2	pounds frozen fish fillets (about 4–6 fillets)
2	tablespoons butter
2	tablespoons oil
2	eggs
1	tablespoon lemon juice
dash	salt
dash	pepper
½	cup flour
½	cup plain bread crumbs

Rinse fish under cold water and pat dry with a paper towel. Sprinkle with salt and pepper. Drizzle with lemon juice on both sides. Blend the eggs and dip fish on both sides. Dredge both sides in the flour, then in the egg again, and lastly in the bread crumbs. In a large skillet, heat the oil and butter. Fry fish on both sides, uncovered, over medium heat for about 20 minutes or until fish turns golden brown.

Grandma's Tip: Fry fish only in a coated frying pan so it will not stick to the skillet. In the process of cooking, drizzle with more lemon juice, if desired. Serve with potato salad, vegetables, and fresh garden salad.

Yield: 4 servings

Fish in Vegetable Stew
(Fisch in Gemüseauflauf)

1–2	pounds fresh or frozen fish fillets
dash	salt
dash	pepper
½	lemon, juiced
3	potatoes
1	onion
1	leek
2	carrots
2	celery stalks
1½	cups beef broth
3	tablespoons finely chopped herbs (parsley, dill, chives)
2	tablespoons margarine

Rinse fish under cold water and pat dry with a paper towel. Cut into 1½ to 2-inch-thick pieces. Sprinkle with salt and pepper. Drizzle with lemon juice. Peel, clean, and cut celery, carrots, leeks, and potatoes into 1-inch-thick chunks. In a pot, melt margarine. Add vegetables, potatoes, and sliced onion. Cover and cook over medium heat for about 5 minutes. Stir in the broth. Layer with fish pieces and sprinkle with finely chopped herbs. Cover and cook over medium to low heat for about 20 minutes or until fish is cooked.

Grandma's Tip: Serve with parsley potatoes, dumpling noodles, or boiled potatoes. If desired, add any other favorite vegetables.

Yield: 3–4 servings

Shrimp with Cocktail Sauce
(Shrimp Cocktailsoße)

½–1	pounds shrimps
3/4	cup sour cream
3/4	cup plain yogurt
1½	tablespoons lemon juice
2	tablespoons ketchup
1	tablespoon dill, finely chopped
1	tablespoon parsley, finely chopped
1	teaspoon mustard
8	salad leaves
2	tomatoes
1	teaspoon mustard
dash	sugar
dash	salt
dash	pepper
1	orange
1	apple

Sprinkle prepared shrimp with salt and pepper. Drizzle with 1 tablespoon lemon juice. In a bowl, blend together yogurt, ½ tablespoon lemon juice, sour cream, ketchup, mustard, dill, parsley, and sugar. In 2 dessert bowls, layer 2 cut salad leaves, ½ diced tomato, and a few diced pieces of the peeled and cleaned apple and orange. Layer with a few shrimp and top each portion with the sauce. Sprinkle with finely chopped dill and parsley.

Grandma's Tip: This cocktail can be used as an appetizer or a light main dish served with toast and butter.

Yield: 4 servings

Herring Salad (Herringsalat)

2	prepared, mid–size herrings, cut into pieces
3	cups water with a dash of salt
1	apple, peeled & diced
3	cooked potatoes
2	tablespoons mustard
6–8	slices of pickles
1½	tablespoons vinegar
3	tablespoons oil
1	cup sour cream or mayonnaise
1	small onion, finely chopped
1	tablespoon parsley, finely chopped
dash	salt
dash	pepper
dash	sugar

In a bowl, combine water and cleaned herring. Cover and set in refrigerator for about half a day. Cut peeled apples and potatoes into cubes, drain herring, and add to apples and potatoes. In a separate bowl, blend mayonnaise, diced pickles, onion, pepper, salt, vinegar, mustard, sugar and oil. Carefully fold sauce into the herring mixture. Before serving, sprinkle with finely chopped parsley.

Grandma's Tip: Boil potatoes shortly before serving so potatoes will be hot. If you live in a state where fresh herring is not available, use about 1 pound herring in a creamed sauce and blend with ½ cup mayonnaise, 3 chopped slices of pickles, ½ diced apple, and ½ sliced onion. As a variation, try sour cream or plain yogurt instead of mayonnaise. Serve with either boiled or parsley potatoes.

Yield: 4 servings

Cod Fish in Wine Sauce (Kabeljau in Weinsoße)

2	pounds cod fish
½	lemon, juiced
1½	onions, sliced
1	cup white wine
3	sliced tomatoes
dash	salt
dash	pepper
2	tablespoons butter
2	tablespoons finely chopped parsley

Drizzle cleaned fish with lemon juice and sprinkle with salt. In a large skillet, melt 1 tablespoon butter. Add fish and wine. Simmer uncovered medium to low heat for about 20 minutes. In a pot, melt 1 tablespoon butter. Add sliced onion and brown over medium heat until light golden. Add sliced tomatoes, sprinkle with salt and pepper, and steam over medium heat for about 10 minutes. Pour steamed onions and tomatoes over fish and steam again over low to medium heat for another 5–10 minutes. Before serving, sprinkle with finely chopped parsley.

Grandma's Tip: To thicken sauce, blend 2 tablespoon water with 1 tablespoon cornstarch and fold into the sauce. Serve with fresh boiled parsley potatoes or rice.

Yield: 4 servings

Chapter 12
Fruit Salads, Purees and Other Desserts

Chapter 12
Fruit Salads, Purees
& Other Desserts

Frucht Salate, Purees und andere Desserts

Apple Salad 1 (*Apfelsalat 1*)

    4   apples, washed and peeled
    ½   lemon, juiced
    1   tablespoon cinnamon
    1   tablespoon sugar
    2   tablespoons raisins

In a mixing bowl, shred apples. Immediately drizzle with lemon juice. Mix sugar and cinnamon together and sprinkle over apples. Add raisins and carefully mix together.

Grandma's Tip: For a richer salad, add about 4 tablespoons liquid whipping cream and sprinkle with nuts.

Yield: 3–4 servings.

Apple Salad 2 (Apfelsalat 2)

    4   apples, washed but unpeeled
    ½   cup plain yogurt or liquid whipping cream
    1   tablespoon honey
    1   tablespoon chopped nuts

Cut apples into small slices. Blend honey with yogurt or whipping cream and carefully mix together with apples. Sprinkle with nuts.

Grandma's Tip: Add 1 peeled and finely chopped orange. Instead of using liquid whipping cream, try whipping the cream first.

Yield: 3–4 servings

Apple Salad 3 (with cooked apples) (Apfelsalat 3)

    4   apples
    2   tablespoons raisins
  2–3   sticks cinnamon
    1   teaspoon vanilla extract
   1½   tablespoons sugar
    1   tablespoon chopped almonds or nuts
    2   cups water

Wash and cut apples into slices; remove core and seeds. Use apples with or without the peeling. In a saucepan, bring to a boil water, apples, sugar, vanilla extract, cinnamon sticks, and raisins to a boil. Reduce heat to low and simmer for about 15 minutes. Set aside until cooled and, before serving, sprinkle with chopped almonds or nuts.

Grandma's Tip: If you want the apples sweeter, add more sugar. Cinnamon sugar is great, too.

Yield: 3–4 servings

Apples in Vanilla Sauce (Äpfel in Vanillesoße)

6	apples
2	tablespoons butter
4	tablespoons sugar
2	cups water
2	cups milk
1½	tablespoons vanilla extract
3	tablespoons raisins
1	tablespoon cornstarch
1	egg yolk

Wash and peel apples, remove seeds and cut into pieces. In a pot, bring water to a boil with 1 tablespoon sugar and ½ tablespoon vanilla extract. Add the apples and simmer at medium heat for about 20 minutes or until tender. Strain apples, sprinkle with raisins, and set aside. In a separate pot, bring 1½ cups milk to a boil with 1 tablespoon vanilla extract and 3 tablespoons sugar. Meanwhile, blend cornstarch with ½ cup milk and add to the other boiling milk. Stir constantly. Stir the egg yolk with the butter and pour over the apples.

Grandma's Tip: Instead of using vanilla extract, try almond extract. To refine, sprinkle with almond slices.

Yield: 4 servings

Applesauce (Apfelmus)

4–5 apples
1 cup water
1 teaspoon vanilla extract
1 tablespoon lemon juice
2 tablespoons sugar
2 cinnamon sticks

Wash and peel apples, remove seeds, and cut into pieces. In a pot, bring water with lemon juice, cinnamon sticks, sugar, vanilla extract, and apples to a boil. Reduce heat to medium and cook until apples are tender. Remove cinnamon sticks and mash everything with a potato masher. To make apple-sauce creamier, blend apple mash again with an electric mixer.

Grandma's Tip: For variety, add 1–2 tablespoons of cinnamon sugar. Instead of mashing apples, you could also press apples through a strainer.

Yield: 4 servings

Apple Casserole (Apfelauflauf)

4–5 apples
3 tablespoons butter
3 tablespoons sugar
3 tablespoons chopped almonds or other nuts
3/4 cup milk
2 egg yolks
2 teaspoons vanilla extract
¼ cup raisins
2 tablespoons cinnamon sugar
1 tablespoon cornstarch

Preheat oven to 320 degrees. Wash apples, remove seeds, and cut into 1 inch thick slices. In a greased casserole dish, combine apples with sugar, almonds, and raisins. Bake the apples in a preheated oven for about 10 minutes or until tender. Meanwhile, in a mixing bowl, blend the egg yolk with vanilla extract, cornstarch, cinnamon, milk, and sugar. Take apples out of oven, pour into egg/milk mixture over the top, and bake for another 5 minutes.

Grandma's Tip: Soak raisins in about 2 tablespoons rum or rum extract and add to apples. Instead of using vanilla extract, try almond extract.

Yield: 4 servings

━━━━━━━━ ⊰•••€€€••⊱ ━━━━━━━━

Filled Pears (Gefüllte Birnen)

    4   pears
    8   salad leaves
    ½   lemon, juiced
  4–5   plums or 8–10 raspberries
    8   ounces cream cheese
    ¼   cup cranberry juice
    ¼   cup plus 2 tablespoons sugar

Wash and cut pears in half, remove seeds, and make a well in the center of each pear half. Set each pear on one salad leaf and drizzle with lemon juice. Meanwhile wash plums, remove pit, cut in small pieces, and fill in the center of the pear. If desired, use raspberries instead of plums. Sprinkle with sugar. With a fork, blend to stir cream cheese with cranberry juice and ¼ cup sugar. Pour over pears and sprinkle with chopped nuts.

Grandma's Tip: Instead of using cream cheese, use 1/3 cup liquid whipping cream or 1/3 cup plain yogurt.

Yield: 4 servings

━━━━━━━━ ⊰•••€€€••⊱ ━━━━━━━━

Plum Salad 1 (Pflaumensalat)

1	pound plums
½	lemon, juiced
1	tablespoon grated lemon peel
2	tablespoons chopped almonds
1½	tablespoons raisins
2	tablespoons cinnamon sugar
2	teaspoons rum or ½ teaspoon rum extract

Wash plums, remove pits and cut in pieces. Immediately drizzle with lemon juice. In a mixing bowl, combine plums with grated lemon peel, almonds, raisins, and rum or rum extract. Carefully mix together and sprinkle with cinnamon sugar.

Grandma's Tip: For a richer salad, add 3 tablespoons liquid whipping cream. Serve with whipped cream.

Yield: 3–4 servings

Plum Salad 2 (Pflaumensalat 2)

1	pound fresh plums
3/4	cup water
1	tablespoon sugar
2	tablespoons cinnamon sugar
1	tablespoon raisins
1	teaspoon vanilla extract

Wash plums, remove pits, and cut into pieces. In a large saucepan, bring water with sugar, vanilla extract, raisins, and plums to a boil. Reduce heat, simmer for about 15 minutes. Remove from heat and cool for about 10 minutes. Sprinkle with cinnamon sugar.

Grandma's Tip: Try cooking 2 cinnamon sticks with the plums. Serve with whipped cream.

Yield: 3–4 servings

Plum Jam and Bread Spread (Pflaumenmus)

3	pound fresh blue plums
1	cup water
1	cup sugar
½	cup raisins
2	tablespoons cinnamon
2	tablespoons finely chopped lemon peel

Wash plums, cut into halves, and remove pits. In a large pot, simmer plums with 1 cup water, sugar, raisins, cinnamon, and lemon peel. Simmer everything for about 1½–2 hours or until plums get mushy and water dissolves. Frequently stir and mash with a potato masher. Pour puree in stoneware or casserole dish and bake in a preheated 300 degree oven for about 15 minutes.

Grandma's Tip: Store in a stoneware container in a cool place. Plum puree is a great bread spread.

Fruit Salad (Fruchtsalat)

2	pound fresh fruit (apples, pears, plums, peaches, oranges, berries, bananas, or any fruit you like)
1	lemon, juiced
2	tablespoons chopped nuts
¼	cup liquid whipping cream
3	tablespoons sugar
2	tablespoons raisins
3	tablespoons grated chocolate

Cut washed and cleaned fruits into pieces and drizzle with lemon juice. In a mixing bowl, combine fruits with whipping cream, sugar, raisins, grated chocolate, and nuts. Carefully mix together.

Grandma's Tip: For variety, soak raisins in about 2 tablespoons rum or 1 tablespoon rum extract plus 1 tablespoon water.

Yield: 4–5 servings

Hot Apple Puree (Apfel Puree)

    6   apples
    1   tablespoon lemon extract
    1   tablespoon lemon juice
    4   cups plus 4 tablespoons water
    2   tablespoons cinnamon sugar
    2   tablespoons cornstarch
    3   tablespoons sugar

Wash and peel apples, remove seeds, and cut into small pieces. In a pot, bring water with apples, lemon extract, and 3 tablespoons sugar to a boil. Reduce heat, cook over medium heat for about 15 minutes or until apples are tender. Remove from heat and crush everything with a masher. Mix 4 tablespoons water with the cornstarch or semolina flour and blend into the apple mash. Bring to a boil again. Blend in the lemon juice and simmer over low heat for about 5 minutes. Before serving, sprinkle with cinnamon sugar.

Grandma's Tip: As a variation, use 3 apples and 3 pears instead of all apples. Add raisins, if desired.

Yield: 4 servings

Hot Cherry Puree (Kirschen Puree)

    1½ cups pitted cherries
    2   cups water
    1   tablespoon cornstarch
    ¼   cup sugar
    1½ tablespoons lemon juice
    2   tablespoons cinnamon sugar
    1   cup milk
    2   tablespoons chopped almonds or nuts

In a pot, bring water, cherries, sugar, and lemon juice to a boil. In a mixing bowl, stir to blend milk with cornstarch and slowly stir into boiling cherries. Reduce heat to low and simmer for about 10 minutes. Remove from heat, mash everything with potato masher, and simmer again for 3–5 minutes. Before serving, sprinkle with cinnamon sugar, and almonds or nuts.

Grandma's Tip: Instead of using fresh cherries, you can use canned cherries. Replace 1 cup of water with cherry juice.

Yield: 4 servings

———————— ·········· ————————

Milk Puree with Strawberries
(Milch Puree mit Erdbeeren)

1	cup oatmeal flakes
1	tablespoon cinnamon sugar
3	cups milk
1½	cups chopped strawberries
2	tablespoons sugar
1	tablespoon chopped nuts, almonds, or coconuts

In a large saucepan, bring milk and sugar to a boil and pour over the oatmeal flakes. Cover and set aside for about 1½ hours. Carefully mix together with strawberries. Sprinkle with cinnamon sugar, nuts, almonds, or coconut.

Grandma's Tip: To quicken the process, cook like a regular oatmeal, mix with strawberries, and sprinkle with cinnamon sugar, nuts, almonds, and coconuts. Serve the oatmeal right away.

Yield: 3–4 servings

———————— ·········· ————————

Vanilla Puree with Sweet Dumplings
(Vanille Puree mit süßen Klößchen)

3	cups milk
4	tablespoons sugar
½	tablespoon vanilla extract
2	eggs, separated
1½	tablespoons cornstarch
dash	salt

In a saucepan, bring 2½ cups milk, vanilla extract, salt, and 1 tablespoon sugar to a boil. Meanwhile, separate the eggs. Beat egg whites until stiff and mix in 3 tablespoons sugar. With a teaspoon, scoop up small dumpling-size balls of egg white and simmer in the milk for about 5 minutes. Remove dumplings and set aside. In a bowl, stir to blend ½ cup milk with cornstarch, salt, and egg yolks. Slowly blend into the other boiling milk. Reduce heat and simmer for another 3 minutes. Reduce heat and simmer for another 3 minutes. Before serving, pour over dumplings.

Grandma's Tip: Instead of using vanilla extract, try an almond extract.

Yield: 3–4 servings

Fresh Berries Gelatin (Beeren Grütze)

1½	cup raspberries
1½	cups blackberries
2	cups grape or cherry juice
1	tablespoon lemon juice
5	tablespoons sugar
1	tablespoons cornstarch
5	envelopes plain gelatin

In a pot, bring 1-3/4 cup juice with berries and sugar to a boil. Cover and simmer for 10 minutes. Blend ¼ cup juice with cornstarch and fold with a wire whisk into the berries. Dissolve plain gelatin in ¼ cup water and add to the berry mixture. Drizzle with lemon juice and bring to a boil again.

Simmer for another 3–5 minutes. Rinse a bowl with cold water and fill with the berry mixture. Refrigerate for about 1 hour. Sprinkle with chopped almonds.

Grandma's Tip: This gelatin also makes a great bread spread.

Yield: 3–4 servings

Sweet Rice Pudding (Süßer Reispudding)

1	cup white rice (uncooked)
4	cups milk
2	tablespoons sugar
1	tablespoon vanilla extract
dash	salt
3	tablespoons butter
2	eggs, separated
2–3	cups water

In a heavy saucepan, bring milk, rice, sugar, vanilla extract, and salt to a boil. Reduce heat and simmer for about 15 minutes. or until rice is cooked. Meanwhile, with a wire whisk or electric mixer, blend butter and egg yolk until creamy. Slowly stir into the rice. Beat egg white until stiff and fold into the rice. Pour into a greased stoneware bowl or round casserole dish. In a large pot, bring water to a boil. Set the dish with rice into the water, reduce heat, and simmer for 45 minutes to 1 hour. Remove from water, set aside, and cool for 30 minutes.

Grandma's Tip: Once rice pudding is cooled, drizzle with a strawberry or raspberry syrup.

Yield: 4 servings

Rhubarb Salad (Rhabarbersalat)

    2–3 stalks rhubarb
    ½   cup sugar, or to taste
    ½   lemon, juiced
    1   tablespoon grated and cleaned lemon peel (optional)
    2   cups water

Clean, peel and cut rhubarb into 2-inch thick slices. In a saucepan, bring water, sugar, lemon peel, lemon juice, and rhubarb to a boil. Reduce heat and cook over medium heat for about 10 minutes. Pour into a bowl and cool for 20 minutes.

Grandma's Tip: For variety, simmer about ¼ cup raisins with the rhubarb.

Yield: 3–4 servings

Caramel Cream (Karamelkrem)

    ½   cup sugar
    2/3 cups water
    3   egg yolks
    ½   tablespoon vanilla extract
    1   cup milk
    1   cup liquid whipping cream
    1   tablespoon cornstarch

In a saucepan, brown ¼ cup sugar until golden. In a skillet, bring the water to a boil and pour over the browned sugar. Rapidly stir until sugar dissolves. In a mixing bowl, blend milk, cornstarch, vanilla, ¼ cup sugar, and egg yolk until creamy. Combine with browned sugar water. Stir and bring to a boil again and refrigerate for about ½ hour. In a bowl, blend the whipping cream until stiff and fold into the cream.

Grandma's Tip: To cool faster, split the mixture into 4 separate dessert bowls and cool.

Yield: 4 servings

Chocolate Pudding (Schokoladenpudding)

3/4	cup milk
1	tablespoon cocoa
½	cup grated chocolate
4	tablespoons butter or margarine
4	eggs, separated
1	teaspoon vanilla extract
½	cup sugar
½	cup flour
½	teaspoon salt
3–5	cups water

In a pot, bring milk, cocoa, 1 tablespoon butter, and grated chocolate to a boil, stirring constantly. Reduce heat, add flour and 2 egg yolks, and fold together into a smooth dough. Store in a cool place for about 10 minutes. Meanwhile, in a bowl, blend 3 tablespoons butter or margarine with 2 egg yolks, sugar, salt, and vanilla extract until creamy. Beat egg whites until stiff and carefully fold everything together with the cooled dough. Pour batter into a casserole or stoneware dish. In a large pot, bring water to a boil and set the dish with the chocolate batter in the water. Reduce heat and simmer for about 1 hour.

Grandma's Tip: To refine, sprinkle pudding with chopped almonds. Chocolate pudding tastes great with a hot vanilla sauce.

Yield: 4 servings

Strawberry Cream (Erdbeerkrem)

6	envelopes plain gelatin
2	cups yogurt
2	cups finely pureed strawberries, fresh or canned
¼	cup sugar
1	cup blended whipping cream
¼	cup water
3–4	tablespoons grated almonds

Dissolve gelatin in water. Blend yogurt and strawberry puree together. Fold in gelatin, sugar and almonds, pour into a bowl, and refrigerate for about 30 minutes. Take about 1 cup whipping cream and fold into the strawberry-yogurt cream. Pour into small dessert bowls and refrigerate for another 2–3 hours. Garnish with a dot of whipping cream.

Grandma's Tip: Garnish cream with fresh strawberry halves and sprinkle with chopped almonds.

Yield: 4 servings

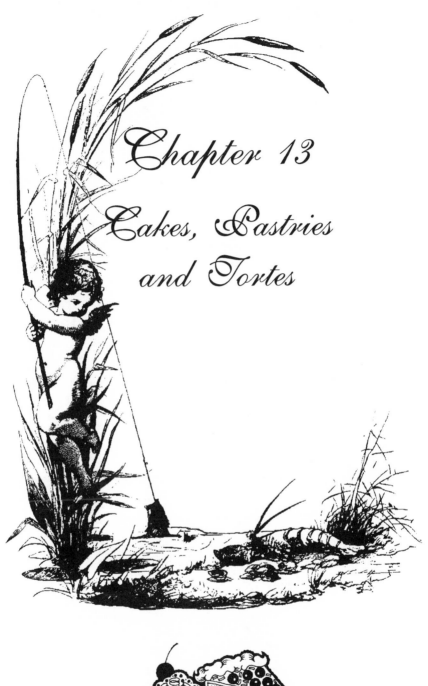

Chapter 13

Cakes, Pastries and Tortes

Chapter 13

Cakes, Pastries, and Tortes

Kuchen, Gebäck und Torten

M ost cakes and pastries are baked in a 350 to 400 degree oven. Cakes are usually baked on the center shelf of the oven, and cookies are usually baked on the upper level.

Especially with cakes, try not to open the door of the oven during the process of baking. If the cake comes into contact with cool air, there is always the possibility that it may fall. To test a cake for doneness, always check with a toothpick first. If dough sticks to the toothpick, the cake is not done yet and needs to be baked a while longer.

Cakes baked in a bundt, springform, or regular cake pan are set aside until they are cooled and then removed from the baking dish. Cakes baked on a flat baking sheet can be removed right away, sometimes with the help of a spatula. To avoid sticking, always grease the pan with butter and sprinkle with either flour or bread crumbs.

To make cake fluffier, sift the flour with baking powder if it is included in the ingredients. When separated eggs are used, make sure that no egg yolk drips into the egg white or the whites will not whip into a stiff cream.

To bake cakes at higher altitudes, lower the temperature. High altitude temperatures are about 320–350 degrees, while regular altitude temperatures are at about 400–425 degrees.

For baking cakes, always use butter instead of margarine.

Cake Fillings (Kuchen Füllungen)

Filling cakes gives them a richer taste and bigger volume. Split cake into 2–3 halves and spread with filling. To prevent the filling from soaking through the cake, spread bottom with a fruit jam or butter first. Cut cooled cake into two halves either with a sharp knife or carefully start cutting with a sharp knife at the desired height and continue separating cake with a thread. Carefully remove top and set aside.

Cream Cheese Filling (Käse-Sahne-Füllung)

4	egg yolks
1	cup sugar
6	envelopes plain gelatin
1	tablespoon lemon juice
1	tablespoon lemon peel
1	teaspoon vanilla extract
18	ounces cream cheese
18	ounces cream, whipped
1	cup milk

In a saucepan, blend gelatin into cold milk. Heat milk and stir. Meanwhile, in a bowl, mix egg yolks with cream cheese, vanilla extract, grated lemon peel, lemon juice, sugar, and heated milk. Fold the milk with dissolved gelatin. Blend together and fold in whipped cream. Cool in the refrigerator for about half an hour and spread on the cake.

Grandma's Tip: For variety, add 2 tablespoons plain raisins or in 1 tablespoon rum-soaked raisins. To make filling creamier, press cream cheese through a strainer before adding to the filling.

Yield: one cake

Buttercream (Butterkrem)

The easiest way to prepare buttercream is to use 2 cups vanilla pudding (use ¼ less milk in preparation) blended with 3 tablespoons butter.

Yield: filling for one cake

Strawberry Cream Filling (Erdbeer-Sahne-Füllung)

    1   pound frozen strawberries
    2   cups cream, whipped
    5   envelopes plain gelatin
    8   ounces cream cheese
    8   ounces sour cream
    1   cup sugar
    2   teaspoons vanilla or almond extract
    2   tablespoons lemon juice

In a bowl, sprinkle strawberries with sugar and thaw. Strain juice into a saucepan and combine with gelatin. Mash strawberries with a potato masher and blend together with sour cream, cream cheese, lemon juice, and vanilla or almond extract. Heat gelatin with strawberry juice and stir into the cream cheese blend. Refrigerate for about ½ hour. Fold in whipped cream.

Grandma's Tip: If you use fresh strawberries, clean and cut about 10–12 strawberries and mash with ½ cup cranberry or other red fruit juice. Save some extra strawberries to garnish the top of the cake.

Yield: one cake

Fresh Berry Filling
(Füllung mit Frischen Beeren)

2 pounds frozen berries (raspberries, cranberries or blackberries)
1½ cups reserved berry juice (add cranberry or grape juice, if necessary)
1 tablespoon lemon peel
1 cup sugar
1 tablespoon lemon juice
1 envelope plain gelatin
½ tablespoon flour
1 tablespoon rum extract

In a bowl, sprinkle berries with sugar and thaw. Strain juice (about 1½ cups, combine with juice if not enough liquid) and pour into a saucepan. Blend in the flour and gelatin and bring to a boil. Remove from heat. Fold in berries, lemon peel, lemon juice, and rum extract. Pour into a bowl and cool for about half an hour in the refrigerator. Use as a filling in between cake layers.

Grandma's Tip: To prevent berries from soaking through the cake, spread first with either 2 tablespoons butter or 2 tablespoons fruit jam.

Yield: 1 cake filling

Cherry-Chocolate Cream Filling
(Kirsch-Schokoladenkrem-Füllung)

2 cups canned cherries without pits
¼ cup cherry juice
¼ cup sugar
1 teaspoon cinnamon
1½ cups cream, whipped
½ cup vanilla pudding
2 teaspoons rum extract
1½ tablespoons cocoa powder
½ tablespoon cornstarch

Strain cherries into a bowl. Save the juice. In a saucepan, heat juice and blend with cornstarch. Fold in cherries, rum extract, sugar, and cinnamon. Set aside. In a bowl, combine whipped cream with vanilla pudding and cocoa powder. Fold into the cherries. Cool in refrigerator for about ½ hour.

Grandma's Tip: To make cherries more flavorful, drizzle strained cherries with about 2 tablespoon rum before preparation. Frost cake with a thick whipped cream and sprinkle with finely grated chocolate.

Yield: filling for one cake

Lemon Cream (Zitronenkrem)

½ cup sugar
3 lemons, juiced
7 tablespoons water
2 envelopes plain gelatin
½ cup cream, whipped
5 eggs, separated
1 teaspoon lemon peel

In a bowl, blend the egg yolks with sugar, lemon juice, and lemon peel until creamy. In a saucepan, blend gelatin into the water. Bring to a boil, stirring continually with a wire whisk. Remove from heat and set aside. Beat the egg yolks until creamy, then add gelatin mixture. With a wire whisk or electric mixer, beat the egg whites until stiff. Fold in the whipping cream, and then the egg yolk cream. Set aside and cool for about 15 minutes.

Grandma's Tip: Before combining cream with egg whites, make sure that cream has already started to gel.

Yield: filling for one cake

Banana Cream (Bananenkrem)

          4   bananas
          ½   cup sugar
      1 ¼   cups milk
          2   eggs, separated
      1 ½   tablespoon cornstarch
          1   tablespoon butter
          1   teaspoon vanilla extract

Mash bananas with a fork or electric blender. In a pot, bring 1 cup milk to a boil. Blend ¼ cup milk with cornstarch and add to the boiling milk. Stir to blend. Add vanilla extract and fold in the egg yolks. Remove from stove. Beat egg whites until stiff and fold banana mash and butter into the cooled milk.

Grandma's Tip: Instead of using egg whites, try 1 cup of whipped cream. To make cream stiffer, fold 1 package plain gelatin into the milk, stirring continually.

Yield: filling for one cake

Cocoa Frosting (Kakaoglasur)

          ½   cup powdered sugar
          2   tablespoons cocoa powder
      3 ½   tablespoons water

In a saucepan, heat water and slowly blend in the sifted powdered sugar and cocoa powder.

Grandma's Tip: To give glaze a mocha taste, mix 4 tablespoons boiling water with 2 tablespoons of coffee grounds. Strain grounds and add to powdered sugar instead of the water. Use only 1 teaspoon cocoa powder instead.

Yield: frosting for one regular bundt cake

Chocolate Cream (Schokoladenkrem)

1¼   cups milk
½   cup sugar
1   tablespoon cornstarch
1½   tablespoons butter
1½   tablespoons cocoa powder or 4 tablespoons grated
        chocolate
1   cup blended whipping cream
½   tablespoon rum extract

In a saucepan, bring to a boil 1 cup milk, sugar, cocoa or grated chocolate, and ½ tablespoon butter. Blend ¼ cup milk with cornstarch and stir rapidly into the boiling milk. Remove from stove. Cool and fold in the rum extract with 1 tablespoon butter and blended whipping cream.

Grandma's Tip: For variety, add 2 tablespoons grated nuts.

Yield: filling for one cake

Lemon Frosting (Zitronenglasur)

½   cup powdered sugar
1½   tablespoons milk (or water)
1½   tablespoons lemon juice

In a saucepan, heat water and lemon juice and slowly stir in the sifted powdered sugar. Spread on the cake and cool.

Grandma's Tip: Instead of using water, try rum or cognac. Instead of using lemon juice, add other syrup or fruit juice for a different taste. Stir rapidly. If glaze becomes too thick, add ½–1 tablespoon water.

Yield: Frosting for 1 regular bundt cake

Note: To make cakes more flavorful and to give them a shinier look, spread cake with frosting. Evenly spread the frosting on the top and/or sides of the cake and set aside for a few minutes to dry.

Basic Raised Cake Dough (Hefeteig)

2¼	cups plus 1/3 cup flour
1	package yeast (¼ ounce)
3/4	cups milk
1/3	cup plus 1 teaspoon sugar
dash	salt
1	teaspoon lemon peel
6	tablespoons butter

Sift 2¼ cups flour with salt into a large bowl. Sprinkle the edge with 1/3 cup sugar, lemon peel and top with butter flakes. In a cup, blend yeast with 1 teaspoon sugar and 1/3 cup warm milk. Make a well in the flour and fill with the yeast and milk mixture. Top everything with 1/3 cup sifted flour, cover bowl with a towel, and set aside in a warm place for about 30 minutes. Knead everything into a dough, cover with a towel again, and set aside for another hour. Sprinkle dough with about 1 tablespoon flour and knead again. On a floured countertop, roll out with a rolling pin into the desired shape.

Grandma's Tip: Dough needs to easily come off hands. If needed, sprinkle with more flour. Sprinkle hands with flour to prevent them from sticking. To get an even batter, poke holes with a fork into the dough before topping. Bake in a preheated 320–350 degree oven at high altitudes, or at 400–420 degrees below 4,000 feet.

Yield: 1 cake baked in a jelly roll pan

Basic Cake Dough with Baking Powder
(Backpulverteig)

2¼	cups plus 1 tablespoon flour
6	ounces butter
1	teaspoon baking powder
dash	salt
1	cup milk
2	eggs
1	teaspoon lemon peel
2/3	cup sugar

Bring butter to room temperature. In a bowl, blend butter with a wire whisk or electric mixer until creamy. Add sugar and blend again. Combine with sifted flour, baking powder, lemon peel, salt, milk, and eggs. Fold everything together. Sprinkle with about 1 tablespoon flour and knead into a dough. Roll out with a rolling pin into the desired shape.

Grandma's Tip: To add more flavor to the dough, combine with 1 teaspoon vanilla or almond extract. After laying out dough into the baking dish, poke holes with a fork to give dough an even shape. Sprinkle hands with flour when kneading the dough. If dough is too sticky, add some more flour. To prevent fruits or other toppings from soaking through the cake, sprinkle dough with bread crumbs first. Bake in a preheated 320–350 degree oven at high altitudes or at 400–420 degrees below 4,000 feet.

Yield: 1 cake baked either in a jelly roll pan or in a spring-form pan.

Mellow Cake Dough (Mürbeteig)

2¼	cups flour
8	ounces butter, cut into cubes and softened
3	tablespoons sugar
dash	salt
2	eggs
1	teaspoon lemon peel or ½ teaspoon lemon juice

On a countertop or large cutting board, sift the flour into a pile. Make a well in the center of the flour and fill with butter and eggs. Sprinkle with sugar, lemon peel, and salt. Fold butter together with eggs, salt, and sugar. Slowly fold in the flour. Sprinkle hands with flour and knead into a dough. If dough is too sticky, add another 1–2 tablespoons flour. Sprinkle flour on a countertop, roll out dough with a rolling pin. Bake in a preheated 320–350 degree oven at high altitudes and at 400–420 degrees at elevations under 4,000 feet.

Grandma's Tip: This dough needs to be prepared in a cool place. Rinse hand with cold water and sprinkle with flour before kneading. Put dough in refrigerate for about 1 hour before baking.

Yield: 1 cake, baked in a jelly roll pan

Shortcake (Tortenboden 1)

2   eggs
6   tablespoons oil
4   tablespoons sugar
6   tablespoons flour
1   teaspoon baking powder

Blend all ingredients together in a bowl. Grease flan pan (thin cake pan with fluted edges) with butter. Pour mixture into pan and bake in a preheated 320 degree oven (high altitude) or in a preheated 400 degree oven (regular altitude) for about 10–15 minutes.

Grandma's Tip: Cool cake for at least 20 minutes. Grease pan with 1 tablespoon butter or margarine and sprinkle with plain bread crumbs to prevent cake from sticking.

Note: This is a thin-layered cake batter for a variety of fruit toppings, also called Bavarian sponge cake.

Yield: 1 flan cake

Flan Cake (Tortenboden 2)

3   eggs
½   cups sugar
¼   cup cornstarch
¼   cup flour

In a bowl, blend eggs with sugar until creamy. Fold in the sifted flour and cornstarch. Grease flan pan (thin cake pan with fluted edges) with butter and bake in a preheated 320–350 degree oven (high altitude) or 400–420 degree oven (regular altitude) for about 10–15 minutes.

Grandma's Tip: Cool cake for at least 20 minutes. Grease flan pan with about 1 tablespoon butter and sprinkle with plain breadcrumbs to prevent cake from sticking.

Yield: 1 flan cake

Kugelhopf Cake (Napfkuchen)

1	cup sugar
9	ounces butter
4	eggs
dash	salt
1	teaspoon vanilla extract
1	tablespoon margarine
2	tablespoons plain bread crumbs
3/4	cup flour
½	cup cornstarch
2	teaspoons baking powder
½	cup milk
2	tablespoons raisins

In a bowl, blend the butter until creamy. Mix in sugar, salt, eggs, sifted flour, vanilla extract, cornstarch, baking powder, and milk. Blend everything into a dough and fold in raisins. Grease baking pan with about 1 tablespoon margarine. Sprinkle with plain bread crumbs and fill with the batter. Bake in a 350 degree preheated oven for about 50–60 minutes (high altitude) or 400 degrees at regular altitude.

Grandma's Tip: Set butter at room temperature for about 15 minutes first so it will be easier to blend. Cool cake for at least 20–30 minutes before removing from cake pan. Sprinkle cooled cake with sifted powdered sugar or spread with a desired frosting. Instead of using plain bread crumbs, baking pan can also be sprinkled with 2 tablespoons flour.

Yield: 1 cake

Loaf Cake (Sandkuchen)

5	eggs
3/4	cup flour
3/4	cups cornstarch
1	cup sugar
1	teaspoon baking powder
1	teaspoon grated lemon peel
4	ounces melted, cooled butter

In a bowl, blend the eggs with sugar for at least 7–10 minutes with an electric mixer until very creamy. While stirring, add sifted flour and cornstarch. Drizzle with butter and sprinkle with lemon peel. Add baking powder and blend again into a dough. Grease a fairly large loaf pan with about 1 tablespoon margarine. Sprinkle with 2 tablespoons bread crumbs. Pour in the batter and bake in a 375 degree preheated oven for about 1 hour (at high altitudes use a 320–350 degree oven).

Grandma's Tip: After baking cake, turn off the oven, open oven door, and leave cake for about 10–15 minutes. Instead of using bread crumbs, sprinkle cake pan with 2 tablespoons flour. Spread cake with desired frosting.

Yield: 1 cake

Bundt Cake with Cream Cheese
(Napfkuchen mit Käsesahne)

1½	cups flour
7	ounces cream cheese
2	tablespoons sour cream
1	teaspoon baking powder
1	teaspoon grated lemon peel
1	tablespoon margarine
2	tablespoons plain bread crumbs
2	tablespoons raisins
4	ounces butter
3/4	cup sugar
2	eggs
dash	salt

In a bowl, blend sour cream with cream cheese until creamy. In a separate bowl, blend the butter until creamy. Add sugar, eggs, cream cheese mixture, lemon peel, sifted flour, baking powder, and salt and mix. Fold in the raisins and blend into a dough. Grease baking pan with 1 tablespoon margarine. Sprinkle with plain bread crumbs so batter won't stick to the pan and fill with the batter. Bake in a 400 degree preheated oven for about 50–60 minutes (350 degrees at high altitude).

Grandma's Tip: Set butter at room temperature for about 15 minutes first so it will be easier to blend. Cool cake at least for 20–30 minutes before removing from pan. Sprinkle with sifted powdered sugar or spread with a desired frosting. Instead of using plain bread crumbs, the baking pan can be sprinkled with 2 tablespoons flour.

Yield: 1 cake

Marble Cake (Marmorkuchen)

1	cup sugar
9	ounces butter
4	eggs
dash	salt
1	teaspoon vanilla extract
1	tablespoon margarine
2	tablespoons cocoa powder
2	tablespoons plain bread crumbs
3/4	cup flour
½	cup cornstarch
2	teaspoons baking powder
½	cup and 2 tablespoons milk
1½	tablespoons powdered sugar

In a bowl, blend butter until creamy. While stirring, add sugar, eggs, vanilla extract, sifted flour, salt, cornstarch, baking powder, and ½ cup milk. Blend everything into a dough and separate into 2 parts. Combine 1 part dough with cocoa powder, 1½ tablespoons powdered sugar, and 2 tablespoons milk. Grease a baking pan with about 1 table-spoon margarine. Sprinkle with plain bread crumbs and, in turns, layer pan with 1 part chocolate dough and 1 part vanilla dough. Bake in a preheated 400 degree oven for about 50–60 minutes (350 degrees at high altitudes).

Grandma's Tip: Set butter at room temperature for about 15 minutes so it will be easier to blend. Cool at least for 20–30 minutes before removing from cake pan. If desired, spread with melted butter and sprinkle with powdered sugar, or spread with frosting and sprinkle with shredded almonds while the frosting is still hot.

Yield: 1 cake

Apple Flan Cake (Apfeltorte)

1	cup flour
2	eggs
2/3	cup sugar
¼	cup milk
1	teaspoon lemon peel
1	teaspoon baking powder
3	apples, cleaned and cut into ½ inch slices
dash	salt
2	tablespoons plain bread crumbs
1	tablespoon margarine
2	tablespoons raisins
3	ounces and 2½ tablespoons butter
½	cup powdered sugar

In a bowl, blend the eggs with sugar and salt until creamy. Slowly fold in the milk and sifted flour with baking powder. Blend in 3 ounces soft butter, raisins, and lemon peel. Grease a springform pan with about 1 tablespoon margarine, sprinkle with bread crumbs, and add the batter. Slightly push apple slices into the batter. Bake in a 400 degree oven for about 45 minutes (320–350 degrees at high altitude). Spread warm cake with 2½ tablespoons butter. Cool the cake and sprinkle with sifted powdered sugar.

Grandma's Tip: Set butter at room temperature for about 15 minutes, so it will be easier to blend. Instead of using bread crumbs, the pan can also be sprinkled with about 2 tablespoons flour. Instead of using powdered sugar, spread the cake with apple jam, sprinkled with shredded almonds, or brush with a lemon icing.

Yield: 1 cake

Butter Cake (Butterkuchen)

1   recipe of basic cake dough (either raised, baking powder or mellow) made with 2¼ cups flour
2   tablespoons margarine
2   tablespoons flour
6   ounces butter
3/4   cups cinnamon sugar

Prepare the basic dough. Grease a jelly roll pan with margarine, sprinkle with flour and roll out the dough into the pan with a rolling pin. Press dough with your fingertips onto the edges of the baking sheet and make a small well every 2 inches. Soften the butter and spread on the cake. Sprinkle with cinnamon sugar and bake in a preheated 375 degree oven for about 30 minutes (320–350 degrees at high altitudes).

Grandma's Tip: To refine, sprinkle with shredded almonds. If dough is too sticky, sprinkle with about 1–2 tablespoons flour before rolling out. At higher altitudes, add a little more flour to make dough firmer.

Yield: 1 cake

Layered Apple or Plum Cake
(Apfel-oder Plaumenkuchen vom Blech)

For the dough:

2¼	cups plus 2 tablespoons flour
2	eggs
5	ounces soft butter
2	tablespoons plain bread crumbs
2	tablespoons margarine
½	cup sugar
1	teaspoon vanilla extract
1	teaspoon baking powder
1	tablespoon lemon juice

Blend soft butter and sugar with electric mixer until creamy. Add sifted flour, baking powder, vanilla extract, eggs, and lemon juice. Knead into a dough. Grease a jelly roll pan with about 2 tablespoon margarine and sprinkle with about 2 tablespoons flour. Add dough and roll out with a rolling pin. Squeeze dough with fingertips onto the edges of the baking sheet. Sprinkle with plain bread crumbs.

For the filling:

12	ounces cream cheese
¼	cup liquid whipping cream
1	package (2–3/4 ounces) vanilla pudding
¼	cup oil
½	cup milk
3/4	cup sugar
1	teaspoon vanilla extract
½	teaspoon lemon juice

Blend cream cheese with liquid whipping cream until creamy. Add sugar and lemon juice. In a saucepan, blend milk with pudding mix and bring to a boil, continually stirring until pudding thickens. Cool the pudding and add to the cream cheese blend. Blend in the oil with the vanilla extract and set aside in refrigerator for about ½ hour.

For the topping:

2	pounds apples, cleaned and sliced
2	tablespoons raisins
2–3	tablespoons sugar

Clean and cut apples into ½ thick slices. Spread filling onto the cake and layer cake neatly with sliced apples row by row. Sprinkle with raisins and sugar. Bake in a preheated 375–400 degree oven for about 45–50 minutes (320–350 degrees at high altitudes for 50–60 minutes. Remove from oven.

For the meringue:
        2   egg whites
        1   tablespoon sugar

Beat the egg white until stiff. Fold in the sugar and evenly spread on the cake. Bake again for another 10-15 minutes or until top turns light golden brown.

Grandma's Tip: Cake will become more solid after cooling for a while. It still tastes great after a few days or when it has been frozen. At higher altitudes, you may need to add some more flour to make the dough firmer.

Yield: 1 cake

Crumb Cake (Streuselkuchen)

1 recipe basic dough (either raised, baking powder or mellow) made with 2¼ cups flour
2 tablespoons margarine
2 tablespoons flour

For the topping:
1-3/4 cups flour
4 ounces melted butter
dash salt
3/4 cups sugar
1 teaspoon cinnamon
2 tablespoons milk

Prepare the basic dough. Grease jelly roll pan with margarine. Sprinkle with flour and roll out the dough with a rolling pin. Press the dough with your fingertips onto the edges of baking sheet. For the topping, combine flour with salt, sugar and cinnamon. Slowly add melted butter and mix into a crumbling dough. To make crumbs fluffier, add more flour. Spread the basic dough with 2 tablespoons milk. Rub flour crumbs between hands and evenly sprinkle onto the dough. Bake in a preheated 375 degree oven for about 25–30 minutes, or at high altitude, in a preheated 320 degree oven for about 30 minutes.

Grandma's Tip: For variety, spread cake with plum jam or butter cream filling, before crumbling the flour on top. At higher altitudes, you may have to add some more flour to make dough firmer.

Yield: 1 cake

Poppy Seed Cake (Mohnkuchen)

For the dough:

1½	cups plus 2 tablespoons flour
2	eggs
5	ounces soft butter
½	cup sugar
1	teaspoon vanilla extract
1	teaspoon baking powder
2	tablespoons margarine
2	tablespoons plain bread crumbs

For the filling:

1	pound finely ground poppy seeds
dash	salt
3½	tablespoons semolina flour or cornstarch
1	teaspoon cinnamon
3/4	cup sugar
2	tablespoons shredded nuts
1–2/3	cups milk
4	tablespoons raisins

In a bowl, mix the butter with sugar until creamy. Blend in the eggs and vanilla extract. Slowly sift the flour with the baking powder and knead into a dough. Sprinkle dough with a dash of flour and knead again. Grease a jelly roll pan with margarine. Sprinkle with 2 tablespoons flour and roll out the dough in the pan with a rolling pin. Squeeze dough with fingertips onto the edges of the baking sheet. Sprinkle dough with 2 tablespoons plain bread crumbs. In a bowl, blend finely ground poppy seeds (grind in a coffee grinder, if necessary) with semolina flour or cornstarch, salt, cinnamon, sugar, and shredded nuts. In a saucepan, bring milk to a boil and pour over the poppy seed mixture. Fold in the raisins, spread onto the dough, and bake in a preheated 375–400 degree oven for about 45 minutes (320–350 degree oven at high altitudes).

Grandma's Tip: For variety, add 2 cleaned and finely chopped apples to the poppy seed mixture and sprinkle the cake after cooling with about ½ cup powdered sugar.

Yield: 1 cake

Shortcake with Fresh Strawberries
(Tortenboden mit frischen Erdbeeren)

For the dough:

2	eggs
6	tablespoons oil
6	tablespoons flour
4	tablespoons sugar
1	teaspoon baking powder
2	tablespoons butter
2	tablespoons plain bread crumbs or flour

For the filling:

2–3/4	ounces (1 package) vanilla pudding powder
2	tablespoons butter
½	cup milk
4	ounces cream cheese
1	teaspoon lemon peel
1	teaspoon lemon juice

For the glaze:

3–4	tablespoons whole berry jam or berry pie filling
2	teaspoons vanilla pudding powder
1	envelope plain gelatin
2	tablespoons water

For the topping:

about 1	pound fresh strawberries
2	tablespoons sugar

For the dough, blend the eggs with sugar until creamy. Add oil and sifted flour with the baking powder. Blend into a dough. Grease a flan pan (thin cake pan with fluted edges) with about 1 tablespoon butter. Sprinkle with about 1 tablespoon plain bread crumbs or flour and add the dough. Bake in a preheated 375–400 degree oven for about 10-15 minutes (320–350 degree oven at high altitudes). Cool the cake and remove from the pan. Spread with 1 tablespoon soft butter and sprinkle with 1 tablespoon plain bread crumbs.

Meanwhile, prepare the glaze. In a saucepan bring 3–4 tablespoons berry jam, 2 tablespoons water, 1 envelope plain gelatin, and 2 tablespoons vanilla pudding powder to a boil, stirring constantly. Remove from the stove and cool for about 10 minutes.

Clean and cut strawberries into halves and sprinkle with about 2 tablespoons sugar.

For the filling, bring ½ cup milk to a boil. Blend in the pudding powder (remove 2 teaspoons for the glaze). Remove from stove. Pour into a bowl and blend with butter. Set aside in refrigerator and cool for about 20 minutes. With an electric mixer, blend in the cream cheese, lemon peel, and lemon juice, and spread on the cake. Neatly place strawberry halves in rows onto the cake. Pour glaze into the center of the cake and carefully spread to the sides.

Grandma's Tip: Instead of using fresh strawberries, try canned peaches or a mixture of sugared raspberries and blackberries. For the glaze, use the fruit juice from canned peaches. Sprinkle the edges of the cake with either coconut or almond slices.

Yield: 1 cake

Glaze 2

3/4   cup fruit juice (cranberry or grape)
2   teaspoons vanilla pudding powder
1   envelope plain gelatin
2   teaspoons cornstarch

In a saucepan, bring all ingredients to a boil. Cool for about 30 minutes. Pour into the center of the cake and slowly spread to the sides.

Yield: enough glaze for 1 cake

Glaze 3

3/4   cup fruit juice
1   package vanilla pudding powder (2–3/4 ounces)
1   teaspoon cornstarch

In a saucepan, bring all ingredients to a boil. Cool for about 10–15 minutes. Pour into the center of the cake and slowly spread to the sides.

Yield: enough glaze for 1 cake

Cream Cheese Bread Loaf

2¼	cups flour
5	ounces plus 3 tablespoons soft butter
1	package ¼ ounces dry yeast
5	tablespoons warm milk
2/3	cup sugar
2	eggs
3	tablespoons raisins
5	ounces creamed cheese
4	tablespoons heavy cream
1	teaspoon vanilla extract
3/4	tablespoon rum extract or 1½ tablespoons rum
dash	salt
¼–½	cup powdered sugar

In a cup, blend dry yeast with 5 tablespoons warm milk and set aside for about 20 minutes. Sift about 2 cups flour on a countertop. Make a well in the center and fill with 5 ounces of almost melted butter, sugar, eggs, yeast mixture, and salt. Knead into a dough and set aside for about 20 minutes. Meanwhile, in a bowl, mix the cream cheese with heavy cream, rum or rum extract, and vanilla extract. Knead with raisins and 1/4 cup flour into the dough. Cover and set aside for another 15 minutes. Form dough into a bread loaf. Cut about ½ inch slice into the middle and put on a greased baking sheet sprinkled with about 2 tablespoons flour. Bake in a 375–400 degree preheated oven for about 45–50 minutes (350 degrees at high altitudes). Remove from oven, brush with 3 tablespoons butter, and sift with powdered sugar. Cool for about 1 hour and serve.

Yield: 1 loaf

Rhubarb Baiser Cake
(Rhabarber Baiser Kuchen)

For the batter:
- 2¼ cups flour
- 3/4 cup powdered sugar
- 9 ounces soft butter
- 1 egg
- dash salt
- 1 teaspoon lemon juice

For the topping:
- 9 egg whites
- 4 pounds rhubarb
- 2/3 cup sugar
- 1 cup powdered sugar
- ½ cup sliced almonds

For the dough, sift flour onto a cutting board or countertop. Fold together with butter. Make a well in the center and add powdered sugar, egg, salt, and lemon juice. Knead into a dough. Set aside in a cool place for about 35–40 minutes. Grease a jelly roll pan with about 2 tablespoons butter and sprinkle with 1 tablespoon plain bread crumbs or flour. Roll out the dough in the pan with a rolling pin. Squeeze dough with fingertips onto the edges of the baking sheet. Bake in a preheated 400 degree oven for about 10 minutes (350 degrees at high altitudes).

Meanwhile, wash and clean rhubarb. Cut into about 1-inch thick pieces. Sprinkle with sugar, set aside, and strain the water.

Blend the egg whites until stiff. Fold in the powdered sugar and blend again with electric mixer or wire whisk.

With the back of a spoon, press shallow wells into the baked cake. Neatly top row by row with rhubarb pieces. Evenly spread with the stiff egg white mixture and sprinkle with almond pieces. Bake for another 15 minutes, in a 400 degree preheated oven (320–350 degrees at high altitude), or until meringue turns light golden brown.

Grandma's Tip: Rhubarb should be sliced and sprinkled with sugar and set aside for at least ½ hour before adding it to the cake. For variety, sprinkle with about 1 tablespoon cinnamon sugar. At high altitudes, you may have to add more flour to make dough firmer.

Yield: 1 cake

Cheesecake 1 (Käsekuchen 1)

For the dough:
1–1/3 cups plus 5 tablespoons flour
1 tablespoon margarine
2 eggs
5 ounces butter
4 tablespoons sugar
½ teaspoon baking powder
dash salt
2 tablespoons plain bread crumbs
1 tablespoon milk or water

For the filling:
4 packages (8 ounces) cream cheese
1 cup milk
1 package (2–3/4 ounces) vanilla pudding
3 eggs
3/4 cup sugar
1 teaspoon grated lemon peel
½ teaspoon lemon juice
1 tablespoons grated almonds
3 tablespoons raisins

For the dough, sprinkle sifted flour with baking powder on a large cutting board or countertop. Layer the edges with soft butter cubes, and sprinkle with sugar and salt. Make a well in the center and add the eggs. With a knife, fold everything together into a dough. Knead dough again. Sprinkle with about 1 tablespoon flour and set aside in a cool place for about 30 minutes. Sprinkle countertop with about 2 tablespoons flour and roll out the dough with a rolling pin. Grease a springform pan with 1 tablespoon margarine, and sprinkle with 2 tablespoons flour. Spread 3/4 of the dough into the pan. With a fork, poke several holes into the dough. Brush sides of springform pan with about 1 tablespoon milk or water and evenly push the other dough around the sides of the pan with fingertips. Sprinkle with 2 tablespoons plain bread crumbs.

For the filling, blend cream cheese and milk with an electric mixer until creamy. Stir in the sugar, eggs, vanilla pudding, grated lemon peel, and lemon juice, and blend everything again. Fold in almonds and raisins. Evenly spread this filling on the dough. Bake in a preheated 400 degree oven for about 50–60 minutes (320–350 degrees at high altitudes).

Grandma's Tip: Cool cake and sprinkle with powdered sugar. To thicken cake, add 2 envelopes plain gelatin to the filling. At high altitudes, add more flour to make dough firmer.

Yield: 1 cake

Cheesecake 2 (Käsekuchen 2)

For the dough:

1–1/3	cups and 5 tablespoons flour
1	tablespoon margarine
1	tablespoon milk or water
2	tablespoons plain bread crumbs
5	ounces soft butter
2	eggs
4	tablespoons sugar
dash	salt
½	teaspoon baking powder

For the filling:

12	ounces creamed cheese
4	tablespoons sour cream
4	tablespoons milk
6	envelopes plain gelatin
1	tablespoon lemon peel
4	egg yolks
3	tablespoons raisins
1¼	liquid whipping cream
1	teaspoon lemon juice
½	cup powdered sugar
2	tablespoons sugar
1	teaspoon vanilla extract

For the dough, sprinkle sifted flour with baking powder on a large cutting board or countertop. Layer the edges with soft butter cubes and sprinkle with sugar and salt. Make a well in the center and add the egg. With a knife, fold everything together into a dough. Knead dough again and sprinkle with about 1 tablespoon flour. Set aside in a cool place for about 30 minutes. Sprinkle countertop with about 2 tablespoons flour and roll out the dough with a rolling pin. Grease a springform pan with 1 tablespoon margarine. Sprinkle with 2 tablespoons flour. Spread 3/4 of the dough in the pan. With a fork, poke several holes into the dough. Brush sides of springform pan with about 1 tablespoon milk or water and evenly push the other dough up the sides of pan with fingertips. Sprinkle with 2 tablespoons bread crumbs.

For the filling, blend cream cheese with sour cream, egg yolks, powdered sugar, sugar, lemon peel, lemon juice, and vanilla extract. In a saucepan, heat milk. Stir in the gelatin and blend into the filling. Whip cream until stiff and also fold, with raisins, into the cream cheese filling. Evenly spread this filling on the dough, bake in a preheated oven for about 50 minutes (320–350 degrees at high altitudes).

Grandma's Tip: To refine the cake, beat 1 to 2 egg whites until stiff and spread on the cake about 10 minutes before it is finished baking. Cool cake and sprinkle with powdered sugar. For variety, try this special cheesecake dough:

1–1/3	cups flour
3	tablespoons milk
½	cup oil
5	ounces cream cheese
2	tablespoons liquid whipping cream
1	teaspoon baking powder
1	teaspoon vanilla
½	cup sugar
dash	salt

Combine cream cheese with milk, liquid whipping cream, sugar, vanilla, salt, and oil. Sift half the flour with baking powder and blend into the cream cheese mixture with an electric mixer. Sift with the rest of the flour and knead into a dough.

Grandma's Tip: Try baking this dough on a flat jelly roll pan, topped with the cream cheese filling. Bake for only 40–45 minutes in a preheated 400 degree oven (320–350 degrees at high altitudes).

Yield: 1 cake

Cheesecake with Cherries (Käsekuchen mit Kirschen)

For the dough:

1–1/3	cups plus 2 tablespoons flour
7	ounces soft butter
½	cup sugar
dash	salt
1	teaspoon grated lemon peel
1	egg yolk
2	tablespoons margarine
1	teaspoon vanilla extract

For the topping:

4	tablespoons soft butter
about	¼ cups flour
4	tablespoons sugar
1	teaspoon cinnamon

For the filling:

3½	packages (8 ounces) creamed cheese
1	package (2–3/4 ounces) vanilla pudding powder
2	eggs
3	ounces melted butter
1	cup milk
1	cup sugar
1	teaspoon lemon juice
1	teaspoon vanilla extract
16½	ounces pitted sweet canned cherries, strained

For the dough, sift the flour on a countertop. Make a well in the center and fill with butter, sugar, lemon peel, egg yolk, vanilla extract, and salt. With a knife, fold everything together. Knead into a dough, sprinkle with 2 tablespoons flour, and set aside in a cool place for about 45 minutes. Grease a springform pan with margarine. Sprinkle with 2 tablespoons flour. Roll out the dough on a floured countertop and spread 3/4 of the dough into the pan. Press dough up the edges of the pan with fingertips. Layer ¼ dough around the edges of the pan.

For the filling, blend cream cheese with eggs, milk, sugar, pudding powder, vanilla extract, and lemon juice until creamy. Fold in melted butter and pour into the springform pan. Layer with strained cherries.

For the topping, blend butter with sugar until creamy. Sprinkle with a dash of cinnamon and fold in the flour. Rub dough between hands and sprinkle over the cream cheese filling. Bake in a preheated 375 degree oven for about 45 minutes (320 degrees at high altitudes). Cool cake for at least 3 hours before cutting into slices.

Grandma's Tip: To prevent the cream cheese filling from soaking through the cake, sprinkle dough first with about 1 tablespoon plain bread crumbs. Fresh pitted cherries can also be used. To refine topping, also sprinkle with 1 table-spoon grated almonds. This cake needs to be cooled for several hours. At high altitudes, add more flour to make the dough firmer.

Yield: 1 cake

Bee-Sting Cake (Bienenstich Kuchen)

For the dough:

2¼	cups flour
4	tablespoons butter
1	package dry yeast
1	cup warm milk
dash	salt
5–6	tablespoons sugar

For the topping:

2/3	cup sugar
4	ounces melted butter
3½	tablespoons milk
8	ounces sliced almonds
4 .	tablespoons honey
2	eggs

For the filling:

2	cups milk
5	tablespoons sugar
1	teaspoon vanilla extract
3	tablespoons cornstarch
4	envelopes plain gelatin
1	egg, separated

For the dough, blend ¼ cup warm milk with yeast and about 1 tablespoon sugar. Set aside for about 20 minutes. Sift flour into a large bowl. Make a well in the center, pour in 3/4 cup milk, melted butter, and 5 tablespoons sugar. Blend together with milk and yeast. Sprinkle with a dash of salt. Knead into a dough, sprinkle with more flour if necessary. Set aside for about 30 minutes in a warm place and let dough rise. Grease a flat baking sheet (jelly roll pan) with about 2 tablespoons margarine. Sprinkle with about 2 tablespoons flour and roll the dough into the pan with a rolling pin. Press dough with fingertips up the edges of the baking sheet.

For the topping, in a saucepan heat butter with honey and sugar. Remove from stove, fold in the almonds, cool, and blend in the eggs and milk. Evenly spread on the dough. Set baking sheet aside for another 20 minutes. Bake in a preheated 400 degree oven for about 25 minutes (350 degrees at high altitudes). Cool cake for about 1 hour.

For the filling, bring 1½ cups milk to a boil. In a cup, blend cornstarch with ½ cup milk, sugar, and vanilla extract. Rapidly stir into the boiling milk. Reduce heat and stir in the egg yolk. Beat egg white until stiff and blend with gelatin into the cooled pudding. Set aside for about 1 hour or until filling thickens. Cut cake into four parts. Cut each part with a sharp knife into 2 layers. Fill the bottom layer with the cooled pudding filling and place second layer with almonds on the top.

Grandma's Tip: For a creamier cake, use twice the amount of filling ingredients. To thicken filling, add about 3 tablespoons vanilla pudding powder.

Yield: 1 cake

Cake Braid (Hefezopf)

         2¼ cups plus 2 tablespoons flour
          6 ounces plus 2 tablespoons soft butter
         ½ cup plus 2 tablespoons sugar
        3/4 cup warm milk
       dash salt
          1 package dry yeast
          3 tablespoons shredded almonds
          1 tablespoons grated lemon peel
          4 egg yolks

Blend 1/3 cup warm milk with yeast and 2 tablespoons sugar. Set aside for about 15 minutes. Meanwhile, sift flour into a bowl, and make a well in the center. Add soft butter, rest of the milk, 2 egg yolks, shredded almonds, grated lemon peel, salt, yeast, and milk mixture. Knead into a dough. Set dough aside in a warm place, cover, and let rise for about 20 minutes. Knead dough again, and cut into 3 equal parts. Braid the three strands, beginning in the center and working toward each end. Grease a baking sheet with about 2 tablespoons butter and sprinkle with 2 tablespoons flour. Place braid on the greased baking sheet and set aside for another 20 minutes. Blend 2 egg yolks and spread evenly on the braid. Bake in a preheated 375 degree oven for about 45–50 minutes (320–350 degrees at high altitudes).

Grandma's Tip: After cooling the cake, spread with a lemon icing. Dough can also be filled with a poppy seed filling. Instead of cutting into 3 pieces, leave the cake in 1 piece. Roll dough on a floured countertop with a rolling pin and fill with a poppy seed cream filling:

        ½ pounds ground poppy seeds
      dash salt
         2 tablespoons semolina flour or cornstarch
        ½ teaspoon cinnamon
        ½ cup sugar
         1 cup milk
         1 tablespoon shredded nuts
         3 tablespoons raisins

In a bowl, blend poppy seeds with semolina flour or corn-starch, salt, cinnamon, sugar, and shredded nuts. In a saucepan, bring milk to a boil and pour over the poppy seed mixture. Blend everything together and fold in the raisins. Fold the edges of dough about 2 inches to the inside over the poppy seed filling, roll and form into the shape of a loaf. Place on a greased baking sheet and bake at the same temperature as the braid for about 55–60 minutes.

Yield: 1 cake

Seasoned Onion Cake (Zwiebelkuchen)

For the dough (baked on a flat baking sheet):
- 2¼ cups plus 2 tablespoons flour
- 1 package dry yeast
- 4 tablespoons softened butter
- 2 tablespoons margarine
- 1 cup milk
- 1 teaspoon salt
- 1 teaspoon paprika

For a thinner layered cake, use half of the dough ingredients.

For the topping:
- 2 pounds onions
- 2 eggs
- ¼ pounds finely cubed bacon
- 1 cup sour cream
- dash salt
- dash paprika
- 2 tablespoons flour
- 4 tablespoons margarine
- 1 teaspoon caraway seeds

In a cup, blend 1/3 cup warm milk with dry yeast and set aside for about 20 minutes. Meanwhile, sift flour into a bowl. Make a well in the center, fill with butter, remainder of the milk, and yeast mixture. Sprinkle with salt and paprika and knead into a dough. Cover and set dough aside in a warm place for about 20 minutes. Grease a baking sheet with about 2 tablespoons margarine. Sprinkle with 2 tablespoons flour and roll out dough into the pan with a rolling pin. With fingertips, press dough onto the edges of the baking sheet. Set aside for about 20 minutes.

In a skillet, brown the bacon cubes. Strain the grease and blend with margarine. Cut onions into fine pieces and brown in the grease until light golden. In a bowl, blend sour cream with eggs, flour, caraway seeds, salt, and paprika. Slowly stir into the onions and pour this mixture onto the cake. Bake in a preheated 375 degree oven for about 50–60 minutes (320–350 degrees at high altitudes).

Grandma's Tip: Instead of using a topping of onions, try ½ pound bacon, 4 tablespoons margarine, 1 cup sour cream, 3 eggs, dash salt, 2 tablespoons cornstarch, and 2 tablespoons caraway seeds, prepared in the same way as the above recipe. At higher altitudes, you may need to add some more flour to make the dough firmer.

Yield: 1 cake

Waffles (Waffeln)

1½	cups liquid whipping cream
3	tablespoons soft butter or margarine
2/3	cup water
2/3	cup flour
dash	salt
½	teaspoon lemon juice
½	teaspoon vanilla extract
½	teaspoon baking powder

In a bowl, blend flour with baking powder, water, and salt. Beat whipping cream until stiff and fold into the flour mixture. Set aside for about 45 minutes. In a saucepan, melt butter. Combine with lemon juice, vanilla extract, and the other ingredients. Grease waffle maker with 1 tablespoon margarine. Fill with about 2½ tablespoons dough and bake for about 3 minutes or until light golden brown.

Grandma's Tip: Either sprinkle waffles with powdered sugar or top with a cherry filling and whipping cream.

Cherry Filling:

16½	ounces canned pitted cherries
2	tablespoons flour or vanilla pudding powder

In a saucepan, bring cherries with liquid to a boil, blend in flour or vanilla pudding powder and cook for two minutes. Serve with waffles and blended whipping cream.

Yield: about 10–12 waffles

Chapter 14

Cookies

Chapter 14

Cookies

Plätzchen

Basic Cookie Dough
(Grundrezept für Plätzchen)

1¼	cups flour
2	ounces soft butter or margarine
½	cup sugar
dash	salt
2	eggs
¼	cup milk
1	teaspoon baking powder

In a bowl, blend butter with sugar, 1 egg, salt, and milk until creamy. Slowly add the sifted flour and baking powder and knead into a dough. Sprinkle countertop with about 2 tablespoons flour and, with a rolling pin, roll out dough about ½ inch thick. Cut out desired shapes. Blend 1 egg and brush onto the cookies. Set cookies on a greased baking sheet and bake in a preheated 320-350 degree oven for about 10–15 minutes, or until light golden brown.

Grandma's Tip: For variety, sprinkle with sugar before baking or make a well in the center of each cookie and top with either a whole hazelnut or a ¼ teaspoon desired jam. Cookies can be brushed, after cooling, with a lemon or cocoa icing and topped with candy sprinkles. At higher altitudes, you may have to add some more flour to make a firm dough.

Mellow Cookies (Mürbeteigplätzchen)

    1–1/3 cups flour
        5 tablespoon sugar
        1 teaspoon vanilla extract
        1 teaspoon lemon peel
        1 egg
       1½ ounces soft butter

Sift flour on a countertop. Make a well in the center. Fill with the egg. Sprinkle the edges with sugar and lemon peel. Drizzle with vanilla extract and top each side with a table-spoon soft (almost melted) butter. With a knife, fold every-thing together, knead into a dough, and set in a cool place for about 30–40 minutes. With a rolling pin, roll out dough about ¼ inch thick on a floured countertop and cut into desired shapes. Place on a greased baking sheet and bake in a preheated 350 degree oven for about 10–15 minutes (320 degrees at high altitudes) or until cookies turn light golden brown.

Grandma's Tip: To give cookies a better taste, blend about 2 eggs and brush a little on each cookie. After cookies are cooled, sprinkle with powdered sugar or brush with lemon or cocoa frosting. At high altitudes, you may have to add more flour to make the dough more firm.

Aniseed Cookies (Anisplätzchen)

    1–1/3 cups sugar
    1–1/3 cups flour
       1½ teaspoons aniseed extract
       3½ tablespoons cornstarch
        4 eggs
        2 tablespoons margarine
        3 tablespoons flour

In a bowl, beat the eggs with sugar until very creamy. Add sifted flour, cornstarch, and aniseed extract. Blend again. Grease a baking sheet with margarine and sprinkle with 3 tablespoons flour. Scoop about 1–1½ tablespoons dough every inch on the baking sheet and set aside for about half a day. Bake over low heat in a preheated 320 degree oven for about 10–15 minutes or until light golden brown.

Grandma's Tip: Place cookies on the baking sheet with the help of 2 teaspoons.

Almond Cookies (Mandelplätzchen)

1-1/3	cups flour
5	tablespoons powdered sugar
dash	salt
7	ounces soft butter or margarine
½	teaspoon grated lemon peel
2	egg yolks
½	tablespoon water
7–8	tablespoons fruit jam (apricot or orange)
about	2–3 ounces sliced almonds

In a bowl, combine flour, powdered sugar, salt, lemon peel, and soft butter or margarine. Knead into a dough. On a floured countertop, roll out the dough with a rolling pin about ¼ inch thick and cut out cookies with a cookie cutter. In a cup, blend the egg yolks with ½ tablespoon water and brush on half the cookies. Layer egg yolk brushed cookies with almond slices. Bake all cookies, in a preheated 375 degree oven for about 10–15 minutes or until light golden brown (350 degrees at high altitudes). Cool cookies. Spread the cookies without almonds with some jam and set the almond topped cookies on top.

Grandma's Tip: Slightly push almond slices with fingertips into the dough so they will not fall off after baking. At higher altitudes, you may have to add some more flour to make the dough firmer.

Coconut Macaroons 1 (Kokos Markronen)

4	egg whites
10	tablespoons powdered sugar
1-3/4	cups shredded coconut
1½	teaspoons vanilla extract
dash	salt

Beat the egg whites with salt until stiff. Slowly add the powdered sugar, vanilla extract, and shredded coconut. Fold together and set aside for 20 minutes. Grease a baking sheet with 2 tablespoons margarine. Scoop 1 full tablespoon batter onto a greased baking sheet and bake in a preheated 320–350 degree oven for about 15–20 minutes or until light golden brown.

Grandma's Tip: As a variation, set batter on small round oblaten wafers and bake. Set cookies on the baking sheet with the help of 2 teaspoons. Cool cookies before removing from the baking sheet.

Coconut Macaroons 2 (Kokos Markronen)

1	cup sugar
2	ounces soft butter or margarine
4	egg whites
½	teaspoon baking powder
1	cup shredded coconut
1	cup flour
dash	salt
1	teaspoon vanilla extract

Blend butter or margarine with the sugar and vanilla extract until creamy. In another bowl, blend the egg white with salt until stiff and add to the butter mixture. Mix baking powder with coconut and flour. Slowly fold into the other ingredients. Grease a baking sheet with 2 tablespoons margarine. Scoop about 1–1½ tablespoons coconut batter at one-inch intervals, on the baking sheet and bake in a preheated 375–400 degree oven for about 10 minutes (320–350 degrees at high altitudes) or until light golden brown.

Grandma's Tip: To refine, place macaroons on small round oblaten wafers. Place cookies on the baking sheet with the help of 2 teaspoons. Cool cookies before removing from the baking sheet.

--------◆◆◆◆◆◆◆◆◆◆--------

Biscuit Cookies (Biskuitplätzchen)

½	cup plus 2 tablespoons flour
4	tablespoons cornstarch
4	eggs, separated
½	cup sugar
2	tablespoons margarine
1	teaspoon lemon peel
dash	salt

In a bowl, beat egg yolks with salt, sugar, and grated lemon peel until creamy. Beat the egg whites until stiff and fold into the creamy egg yolk mixture. Stir in flour sifted with cornstarch and blend again. Grease a baking sheet with about 2 tablespoons margarine. Sprinkle with 2 tablespoons flour and place spoonfuls of cookie dough every 1½ inches on the baking sheet. Bake in a preheated 375 degree oven for about 15 minutes (350 degrees at high altitudes) or until light brown.

Grandma's Tip: After cooling cookies, sprinkle with powdered sugar or brush with a desired icing.

--------◆◆◆◆◆◆◆◆◆◆--------

Cookie Macaroons (Plätzchen Makronen)

For the cookie dough:
- 3   egg yolks
- 1   tablespoon lemon peel
- ½   cup powdered sugar
- 4   ounces soft butter
- 1   teaspoon vanilla extract
- 1   cup plus 2 tablespoons flour

For the topping:
- 2/3   cup powdered sugar
- 3   egg whites
- 3/4   cup grated almonds
- 1   teaspoon cinnamon
- ½   teaspoon vanilla extract

For the cookie dough, sift flour on a countertop. Make a well in the center. Add the egg yolks, lemon peel, powdered sugar and vanilla extract. Set soft butter cubes on the edges and fold with a knife together. Knead into a dough. Sprinkle with about 1 to 2 tablespoons flour and set aside in a refrigerator for about 30 minutes.

For the macaroon topping, beat the egg whites until stiff. Add cinnamon, vanilla extract, powdered sugar, and almonds and fold into a dough.

Sprinkle countertop with about 3 tablespoons flour. With a rolling pin, roll out the cookie dough ½ inch thick and cut with a sharp knife into equal rectangles. Grease a baking sheet with about 2 tablespoons margarine. Spoon cookies onto the baking sheet and bake in a preheated 350 degree oven for about 5 minutes. Remove from oven, top each cookie with 1 tablespoon macaroon batter and bake for another 10–15 minutes or until light golden brown.

Grandma's Tip: If dough needs to be firmer and easier to roll out, sprinkle with some more flour. Shape macaroon topping with the help of 2 teaspoons.

Cinnamon Stars (Zimtsterne)

3	ounces soft butter or margarine
3½	tablespoons honey
1	teaspoon cinnamon
½	cup plus 5 tablespoons sugar
4	tablespoons grated nuts
1	egg
1	teaspoon baking powder
1	cup apple juice
1¼	cups flour

In a bowl, blend butter or margarine with 5 tablespoons sugar until creamy. Add cinnamon, honey, flour sifted with baking powder, egg, apple juice, and grated nuts. Knead into a dough. Sprinkle countertop with about 1/2 to 3/4 cup sugar. Sprinkle dough with 2 tablespoons flour and roll out over the sprinkled sugar until about ½ inch thick. Cut out star-shaped cookies and set aside for 30 minutes. Grease baking sheet with 2 tablespoons margarine. Set cookies on the baking sheet and bake in a preheated 350 degree oven for about 10 minutes or until light golden brown.

Grandma's Tip: To refine cookies, brush with a lemon or other desired icing. At higher altitudes, you may have to add some more flour to make the dough firmer.

Vanilla Crescent Cookies (Vanillekipferl)

For the dough:
- 3/4 cup flour
- ½ cup grated almonds
- 4 ounces soft butter
- 1 teaspoon vanilla extract
- 3 tablespoons sugar
- dash salt
- 1 egg yolk
- 2 tablespoons margarine

For the topping:
- ½ cup powdered sugar

In a bowl, blend butter with sugar and egg yolk until creamy. Add sifted flour, vanilla extract, salt and grated almonds and knead into a dough. Set aside in the refrigerator for about 40–50 minutes. Form dough into finger-thick rolls, and shape into 2-inch-long half-moons. Grease a baking sheet with 2 tablespoons margarine. Place cookies on the baking sheet and set aside for another 30 minutes. Bake in a 350 degree oven for about 10–15 minutes (320 degrees at high altitudes) until light golden brown. Sprinkle a cutting board or countertop with the powdered sugar, drizzle with vanilla extract, and fold together with a knife. Dip warm vanilla cookies with top side down in the icing and cool.

Grandma's Tip: Dip cookies, after cooling, into powdered sugar. Shape cookies into a half moon with fingertips. At higher altitudes, you may have to add a little more flour to make the dough firmer.

Hazelnut Cookies (Haselnussplätzchen)

        5   tablespoons flour
        ½   cup sugar
        5   ounces soft butter or margarine
        1   teaspoon vanilla extract
        1   egg yolk
        4   ounces grated hazelnuts
        ½   teaspoon baking powder

In a bowl, blend soft butter with sugar, vanilla extract, and egg yolk until creamy. Slowly fold in the sifted flour with baking powder. Add hazelnuts and blend again. Place dough into a piping bag (cookie press) and press dough about 2 inches long each on a greased baking sheet. Bake in a preheated 375 degree oven for about 15 minutes or until light golden (350 degrees at high altitudes).

Grandma's Tip: Dough also can be squeezed through a Ziplock bag with a small hole cut in the bottom. For variety, melt 1 cup of chocolate pieces and brush on the cooled cookies.

Fine Blended Cookies *(Sandgebäckplätzchen)*

2/3 cup flour
2/3 cup cornstarch
  1 teaspoon vanilla extract
  5 ounces soft butter
2/3 cup sugar
  1 egg

In a bowl, blend butter, sugar, and the egg until very creamy. Add vanilla extract, sifted flour, and cornstarch. Blend again. Place in a piping bag (cookie press) and press 2-inch-long, S-shaped cookies on a greased baking sheet. Bake in a pre-heated 350 degree oven for about 10–15 minutes or until light golden brown.

Grandma's Tip: Instead of using a cookie press, a Ziplock bag can also work. Cut a small hole in a corner of the bag and fill with dough. To refine, dip ½ of the cookies, after cooling, into melted chocolate.

Index

Index of English Titles

Spices

Spreads for Sandwiches

Salads

Salads with Cooked Vegetables

Soups

Sauces

Potatoes

Breakfast Foods

Vegetables

Meat Dishes

Index of German Titles

Order Form
The Best of Grandmother's German Cookery

Please complete the following form
and mail with payment to:
C. Werl-Graves
P.O. Box 26144
Colorado Springs, Colorado 80936-6144

Please send me _____ copies of the *Best of My Grand-mother's German Cookery* at $16.95 each plus $2.95 postage and handling (for a total of $19.90) per book. Please make check or money order payable to "C. Werl-Graves". Thank you for your order . . . and Happy Cooking!

Name _____

Street _____

City _____ State ____ Zip_____

Please complete the following form
and mail with payment to:
C. Werl-Graves
P.O. Box 26144
Colorado Springs, Colorado 80936-6144

Please send me _____ copies of the *Best of My Grand-mother's German Cookery* at $16.95 each plus $2.95 postage and handling (for a total of $19.90) per book. Please make check or money order payable to "C. Werl-Graves". Thank you for your order . . . and Happy Cooking!

Name _____

Street _____

City _____ State ____ Zip_____